English Language Learners

Teaching Strategies that Work

Larry Ferlazzo

 LINWORTH

AN IMPRINT OF ABC-CLIO, LLC
Santa Barbara, California • Denver, Colorado • Oxford, England

Library of Congress Cataloging-in-Publication Data

Ferlazzo, Larry.
  English language learners : teaching strategies that work / Larry Ferlazzo.
    p. cm.
  Includes index.
  ISBN 978-1-58683-524-8 (alk. paper) — EISBN 978-1-58683-525-5 (ebook)
1. English language—Study and teaching (Middle school)—Foreign speakers.
2. English language—Study and teaching (Secondary)—Foreign speakers.
3. Multilingualism in children.   4. Content area reading.   I. Title.
  PE1128.A2F45   2010
  428.2'4—dc22   2010002118

ISBN: 978-1-58683-524-8
EISBN: 978-1-58683-525-5

14 13 12 11 10   1 2 3 4 5

This book is also available on the World Wide Web as an eBook.
Visit www.abc-clio.com for details.

Linworth
An Imprint of ABC-CLIO, LLC

ABC-CLIO, LLC
130 Cremona Drive, P.O. Box 1911
Santa Barbara, California 93116-1911

This book is printed on acid-free paper ∞

Manufactured in the United States of America

Contents

Figures

About the Author

LARRY FERLAZZO has taught English and social studies—primarily to English language learners—at Luther Burbank High School in Sacramento for six years. Prior to becoming a teacher, he spent 20 years working as a community organizer assisting low- and moderate-income families improve their communities. He has won numerous awards, including the Leadership for a Changing World award from the Ford Foundation, the International Reading Association Presidential Award for Reading and Technology, and the Sacramento State College of Education's Education Partnership Award. He writes a blog for teachers about working with English language learners (<http://larryferlazzo. edublogs.org/>) and has a Web site for students (<http://larryferlazzo.com/>). He is also the author (with Lorie Hammond) of the book *Building Parent Engagement in Schools*.

Acknowledgments

I'd like to especially thank my wife, Jan, for her support while writing this book. In addition, I'd like to thank the administrators (especially Ted Appel, our principal), faculty, staff, parents, and students of Luther Burbank High School for helping me become a better teacher and learner. I'd like to highlight Kelly Young and his mentorship—my skills as a teacher have vastly increased because of what I have learned from him. In addition, I appreciate everything I learned during my community organizing career with the Industrial Areas Foundation. I'd also like to express my appreciation to Kate Vande Brake and Cyndee Anderson from Linworth Publishing for their help and support in developing this manuscript.

Introduction

I was waiting in line for one of the school's copy machines to become available. Another teacher approached me.

"You just got the class of the Hmong students who came from Thailand and have never been in school before, right?" he asked. I confirmed what he said.

"Boy, I can't imagine what that must be like," he continued. "They can't speak a word of English. I bet they can't read their own language, and you probably have to teach them just how to hold a pencil. I wouldn't want to be in your shoes."

"I love the class," I replied. "The students are eager to learn, they've got incredible life experiences, and I'm getting intellectually challenged, big time, on how to connect the two." I went on to share some examples of what we had been doing, including creating models of traditional Hmong and American homes to compare which ones were designed better to keep cooler or warmer; drawing and describing traditional Hmong "story cloths," which told Hmong history; and looking at the differences and similarities between how Native Americans were treated in this country and what the Hmong experience was.

"Wow," the teacher said as he left the copy room. "I wonder how I could get to teach that class next year?"

This book shares practical experiences in looking at teaching English language learners and others through a lens of *assets* and not *deficits*. This perspective draws on my 20 years of being a community organizer prior to becoming a public school teacher, as well as an extensive review of supporting research.

Community organizing is about developing leaders and helping them improve their lives. Organizing is about helping people, many of whom are initially reluctant to participate, learn a *new language* of how to engage in the world and with each other. It is about helping them to use their own traditions and stories to re-imagine themselves and their dreams. It is about helping them tap into their own intrinsic motivation and embark on a journey of action, discovery, and learning. It is about helping them develop the confidence to take risks, make mistakes and learn from them, try new things, and develop a discipline of self-reflection. Importantly, it is about doing these things through enforcing what Saul Alinsky, the father of modern-day community organizing, called the "Iron Rule": *Never do for others what they can do for themselves. Never.* It is about their energy driving this journey. And it is about *the organizer learning* as much as it is about *the organizer teaching*.

These same principles can be effective guides for educators in schools.

Guiding Teaching and Learning Principles

Help students learn a *new language* of how to engage in the world and with each other.

Help students use their own traditions and stories to re-imagine themselves and their dreams.

Help students tap into their own intrinsic motivation and embark on a journey of action, discovery, and learning.

Help students develop the confidence to take risks, make mistakes and learn from them, try new things, and develop a discipline of self-reflection.

Never do for students what they can do for themselves.

This book is focused on converting these principles to concrete actions in schools, which can, as the research in the following chapters shows, mobilize and motivate English language learners in ways we—and they—might never have considered possible. Applying these principles in the classroom can help nonnative English speakers develop faster and deeper command of the English language, higher-level thinking skills, resiliency (the ability to move forward despite hardships and obstacles), and self-confidence—all of which can result in greater levels of academic achievement. Another outcome can be educators becoming more intellectually stimulated and professionally energized. Someone once said that schools are where younger people go to see older people work. That is definitely not the case in classrooms where these principles play a consistent role. The purpose of this book is not to pile on more work for teachers to do. Instead, it will provide suggestions on how to use these principles to help teachers do what they want to do anyway—just in a way that is driven by *student* energy instead of teacher energy.

Using these principles in communities results in dramatic concrete improvements, and the same can happen in schools. But for organizers, the best results are seeing how dramatically people can change *themselves* based on what they learn through community organizing—how to give and receive constructive critique, how to lead and guide diverse groups, how to confidently confront challenges, and how to take the initiative to create change. They can develop a burning desire to learn and can often surprise themselves with their capacity to excel with difficult tasks.

Seeing these kinds of results caused me to wonder how much better people's lives could be if they developed effective leadership skills at a younger age. I wanted to help people learn to think critically and act confidently as they were growing up, rather than waiting until they were adults. This desire, and my belief that many of the organizing strategies that worked successfully with adults could benefit teenagers and younger children, prompted my decision to become a teacher.

Although I had seen these organizing principles work effectively with people from all ethnicities and economic backgrounds (just as I have found the application of these principles to the classroom successful with English language learners and native English speakers alike), I was particularly interested in using them with English language learners. One reason was personal. I grew up in an immigrant household in New York City and believe that experiences I had growing up helped develop my desire to use community organizing, both in and out of school, with newcomers to the United States.

One incident in particular stands out. My Uncle Horace was always spoken of in my family as having been a brilliant child, though a bit rambunctious in school. My grandmother was a new immigrant from Italy who had been deserted by her husband and had three children to support. She didn't really understand what school staff wanted her to do when they met with her about Horace's behavior in the late 1930s. As my father told the story, they brought some papers for her to sign, and told her they wanted to help and send him to a hospital for a short time. Though she didn't necessarily understand, she knew this was America, and figured that these well-meaning school officials only wanted the best for her oldest son.

Horace, like a number of other children who were considered behavior problems at that time, received an experimental lobotomy shortly thereafter, and had to spend the remaining 50 years of his life in a state hospital. It seemed to me that you could see the pain in my grandmother's eyes whenever she spoke of Horace and whenever my father brought him to visit us. I remember the childlike man who was always looking at his watch to ensure he was returned to the hospital on time. I always felt that my grandmother never forgave herself for allowing him to be taken away.

I learned several lessons from this story. People who felt powerless could be intimidated and bullied by those representing institutions of power. Instead, low-income people needed to feel capable and competent in dealing with so-called experts. And newcomers to the United States were even more vulnerable to manipulation because of their unfamiliarity with the English language and American political and legal system.

Years later, my father became a teacher. And though he left it as a full-time job because he felt he couldn't support a growing family on a teacher's salary, it was his first love, and he continued to teach at night. In fact, he taught ESL classes. I remember him coming home late full of energy. He told me once, "Larry, I don't want to teach my students to survive in the United States. I want them to learn to *thrive!*"

After I made a decision to become a classroom teacher, and to focus on working with newcomers, I began to observe classes that had large numbers of English language learners to see what I might be getting myself into. I also began talking with immigrant leaders of our community organization to learn about their classroom experiences, those of their friends, and those of their children. Through these observations and conversations, I developed an even greater determination to see how I could incorporate the principles outlined in this chapter into my teaching.

I saw and learned how older English language learners were often treated in schools. Many teachers taught middle and high school students as if they were little children, using simplistic activities that denigrated the sophisticated reasoning skills and life experiences that young adolescents and teenagers brought to the classroom. Then and now, many educators looked through the lens of a deficit model that focused only on students' limited English skills and not on the wealth of their prior knowledge. Consequently, many students lost interest in school and never discovered how to push past the early frustrations of learning another language so they could continue their education.

In contrast, the following methods can help students become cocreators of their education, without being constrained by their limited English skills. I will explain each in greater detail throughout the book, including their basis in research and many practical examples of how to apply them with students.

Building Strong Relationships with Students

Community organizers often say that "organizing" is just another word for "relationship building." You can quickly identify people's self-interests on the surface, such as the desire to get a better job or buy their own homes. But it is necessary to go deeper and find out what personal experiences might inspire people to seek improvements in order to develop power to create significant personal and social change. These insights can only be uncovered in the context of a genuine relationship.

We can use these self-interests to be more of an *agitator* (challenging students to reflect on their own knowledge, lives, and experiences and then use these reflections to frame a vision for the future) instead of an *irritator* (telling them what they should want to know and how they should learn it). Doing this successfully can help English language learner students fight past the frequent frustrations most people experience in learning a second language.

Accessing Prior Knowledge through Stories

Stories can help immigrant students make connections based on their similar experiences and help them consider alternative perspectives. These classroom conversations involve an exchange of information, not an interview or a one-way presentation, and can result in the creation of a community of learners. By developing this type of class culture, students can find that they have both more personal self-confidence and more in common with each other than they had originally thought. This combination of increased self-assurance and feeling more connected to their peers results in students feeling more comfortable taking risks, which is one of the keys, if not the key, to second language learning success.

Identifying and Mentoring Students' Leadership Potential

Assisting students to develop the leadership skills helps them become cocreators of their learning journey. *Everyone* in the class, including the official educator, can be a learner *and* a teacher.

Patiently helping our students develop the capacity to lead helps them create their own sense of power, which dictionaries define as "the ability to act"—both individually and collectively. Developing this capacity is particularly important to English language learner students, many of whom have been uprooted from their native countries through no choice of their own, face challenges in understanding and communicating in our culture's primary language, and can be living in lower-income communities where examples of powerlessness are obvious each day.

Learning by Doing

It's difficult for students to feel powerful if the leadership and energy only flows from the teacher. Using Saul Alinsky's "Iron Rule" of "never doing for someone what they can do for themselves" as a guide, we can show students how to become much more than empty vessels waiting to be filled by the educator's input.

Community organizers describe action as the oxygen of an organization. Action is equally important to the healthy life of a classroom. We need to help students learn that people without power tend to *react* to rules and experiences that others create, while people with power can act to create those rules and experiences.

Having English language learners describe and interpret classroom experiences has long been considered an effective instructional strategy. Helping students discover knowledge on their own through those experiences instead of telling them information creates even richer language (and life) learning opportunities. To paraphrase Dave Kees, a talented English teacher in China: What makes for more engaging stories and conversation—going on a prepackaged tour or on an adventure?

Reflection

Many of us often define ourselves by our activities instead of the outcomes of those activities. Educators, too, can fall into the trap of substituting busyness for real progress. As T. S. Eliot once said, "We had the experience but missed the meaning."

When we take time to critically review our work and search for evidence of our accomplishments (both through data and personal observation), we learn how to improve and we'll often uncover key lessons we may have missed. It's important for educators and students alike to develop the discipline of reflection. Many often do not take the time to digest what they are doing and learning. English language learner students have to learn double the amount of other students—language *and* content—and are therefore even less likely to naturally incorporate this element. There's always so much to learn!

It's common for many groups doing good work in neighborhoods to focus all their energy on what they view as the task at hand—to build affordable housing, to develop jobs, to provide social services. In community organizing, the task at hand is providing people with the opportunity to develop relationships, relate their personal stories and traditions to what is going on now, develop themselves as leaders, shape their own learning environment, and take time to digest it all.

By focusing on these priorities, community organizing groups, in turn, are often recognized locally and nationally as extraordinarily effective organizations in getting needed services provided to low-income communities, creating affordable housing, and developing jobs that provided good wages and benefits to previously low-income people. The concentration on personal development in the context of "agitational" relationships (see the earlier discussion about the difference between "agitation" and "irritation") can result in people gaining concrete community improvements and, much more significantly, insights and skills that can last a lifetime.

The purpose of this book is to demonstrate that similar outcomes can result by applying the steps described above to English language learner classrooms (*and to other classes as well*). By using these strategies in the classroom, educators can help English language learners make huge strides in their language development *and* in becoming lifelong learners.

Many of the individual classroom practices described in this book may not be especially new to teachers (though some may be used more in mainstream classes than with English language learners). However, the benefits of both these new and not-so-new instructional strategies can be maximized if they are conducted in the context of these five key methods of teaching. These methods offer a framework for teaching English language learners that can be both stimulating and effective to teachers and students alike.

Each Chapter Follows This Format

- ✦ A short, real-life vignette illustrating the concept.
- ✦ What the research says about the concept as it relates to student achievement with English language learners. In addition, there will be short vignettes called "Research in Action" that directly demonstrate research findings.
- ✦ Numerous classroom examples, including several step-by-step lesson guides for multiple lessons, and examples of student work. In addition, an explanation will be included showing how each classroom example fits into the six standards domains the State of California mandates for its English language development (ELD, also known as ESL) classes. Similar standards exist in most other states. To make these standards more easily understandable, a one-sentence description developed for each domain by the Sacramento City Unified School District will be used. These standards are listed in Figure 1, which also includes a chart correlating them to each lesson. In addition, their citation numbers will be listed next to the lessons as they are described throughout the book.
- ✦ How to incorporate technology easily—both as consumers of existing content on the Internet and as creators using Web 2.0 applications The only prior knowledge needed would be knowing how to use e-mail, surf the Internet, and how to copy and paste. In addition to this section, each chapter will also contain several "Tech Tips" specifically related to classroom lessons being discussed. An extensive list of Web resources can also be found in Appendix 1.
- ✦ How to assess if the strategy is working.
- ✦ What might be challenges facing educators who want to implement these strategies and how to effectively respond to them.

Appendix 2 describes classroom games that can be used to support most of the concepts expressed throughout the book.

Educators today live in the world of high-stakes standardized testing, scripted curriculums, and pressured administrators—in other words, a world where compromises sometimes have to be made between what they would like to do and what they are required to do. Organizers often speak about the difference between the world as it is and the world as we'd like it to be. In order to be effective, we need to recognize the tension between the two and understand the importance of compromise. As organizers say, though, we just need to take care that these compromises are more like a half of a loaf of bread and not like cutting a baby in half, as King Solomon proposed.

Though this book is framed in the context of teaching English language learners, I have also used all the teaching and learning strategies that are shared with native English speakers. What I have labeled the "organizing cycle"—building relationships, learning and sharing stories, developing student leadership, learning by doing, and reflection—can function effectively as a universal teaching and learning strategy (though I have given it the "organizing cycle" name, a somewhat similar sequence is used by effective community organizers throughout the world).

In addition, practically all of the lessons that are shared can be differentiated to work well in a multilevel classroom.

I will often use the word "educator" instead of "teacher" throughout this book. The strategies discussed in it can be helpful to anyone involved in the education field—teachers, librarians, other school staff, and parents.

This book is not intended to be a precise road map for educators to follow. Instead, it is meant to be more of a compass for educators to use and more effectively help their English language learner students acquire the English reading, writing, speaking, and listening skills they need to thrive in both academic and community settings; help them become comfortable in a new culture while drawing on the strengths of their native traditions; and assist them to develop the needed skills to participate as active citizens in our democracy.

Use this book to help develop your vision of what you think will give you and your students energy to learn and to teach. Use these ideas to remind yourself to consider what kind of legacy you want to leave with them.

CHAPTER	NAME OF ACTIVITY	CALIFORNIA ELD DOMAIN
Building Strong Relationships with Students	Introductions lesson plan	1,2
	Additional student presentation projects	1,2
	Writing projects	5,6
	Games	1
	Reading projects	2,3,4,6
	Technology projects	1,5,6
Accessing Prior Knowledge through Stories	Immigration unit	1,2,3,4,5,6
	Venn diagrams	5,6
	K-W-L chart	1,6
	Two-part posters	1,2,3,5,6
	Family trees	1,6
	Critical pedagogy lesson plan	1,5,6
	Taking action	1,2,3,6
	Technology projects	1,5,6
Identifying and Mentoring Students' Leadership Potential	Making the qualities of a good learner and leader explicit	1,2,3,4,6
	Democracy in the classroom	1
	Classroom management	1
	"I feel powerful when . . ." lesson plan	1,6
	Learning strategies	1,2,3,4,6
	Teaching others	1,2,3,4,5,6
	Technology projects	1,2,3,4,5,6
Learning by Doing	Picture word inductive model unit plan	1,2,5,6
	Learning phonics inductively	1,2,5,6
	Implementing problem-based learning	1,2,3,5,6
	Implementing voluntary free reading	1,2,3,4,6
	Technology projects	1,2,3,5,6
Reflection	Learning log or reflection journal	1,5,6
	Metaphor or simile student reflection lesson plan	1,5,6
	Other special reflection projects	1,5,6
	Reading and watching about reflection	1,2,3,4,6
	technology projects	1,2,5,6

(Continued)

ENGLISH LANGUAGE DEVELOPMENT STANDARDS
CALIFORNIA ELD DOMAINS

1. Students use English for everyday communication in socially and culturally appropriate ways and apply listening and speaking skills and strategies in the classroom.

2. Students apply word analysis skills and knowledge of vocabulary to read fluently.

3. Students will read and understand a range of challenging narrative and expository text materials.

4. Students will read and respond to literature.

5. Students will write well-organized, clear, and coherent text in a variety of academic genres.

6. Students will apply the conventions of standard English usage orally and in writing.

Figure I.1 Chart showing each lesson and correlating California standards.
Source: Course of Study for English Language Development, Sacramento City Unified School District, 2005, pp. 7–12.

CHAPTER 1

Building Strong Relationships with Students

Ivana was a seventh grader who recently came to West Sacramento from the Ukraine. She had been doing well in our self-contained class of English language learners (ELL) but was feeling frustrated by not being able to remember the past tense of irregular verbs. She ignored my suggestions not to worry about it for now—it would come with time, but it clearly continued to bother her.

She had asked to spend time after school to receive tutoring on this issue one day. Instead of providing direct instruction, I began by asking her a little more about her life—what did her family do in the Ukraine? Why did they come here? What were some of the challenges she and they were facing? What were her interests? She was a little reticent to share at first, but eventually she opened up, especially after I shared that I came from an immigrant family.

"I love ballroom dancing," was one of the things she told me. She had taken years of classes in the Ukraine and couldn't stop talking about it now. She had a short video at home of one of the contests she had participated in when she was living there. "Could I bring it in and show a little of it to you?" she asked. I told her yes as an idea began percolating in my mind.

The next day she showed me the video of her and her partner doing a flawless dance routine. I then shared my idea with her. The day before she had told me about various different dances and their difficulty level. Would she be interested in developing a board game, I wondered, with four different levels mirroring ballroom dances? She could prepare cards with questions about irregular verbs, and have to answer them correctly to advance to the dance levels. She could hardly contain her excitement. She recruited two friends and they spent three days after school planning and decorating a game board and game pieces, and preparing cards. They regularly played the beautifully designed game—the first board game, I would wager, in the history of the world that used ballroom dancing to teach a second language. Ivana gained more confidence in her English and became less concerned about having to get every irregular verb perfect. Other students in the class then decided they wanted to make their own board game, too.

Ivana had hit a roadblock. Instead of focusing initially on the *task* of remembering verb tenses (and, as a second-language-learner of Spanish, I certainly remembered how numbingly awful that experience could be), I spent time developing a *relationship*. I began developing that relationship by asking questions about Ivana's life and sharing about my own. It was not a one-way interview—it was an *exchange*. A new tactic—the ballroom dancing board game—that helped Ivana respond to her challenge came out of this relationship-building experience, and she took ownership of it.

What Do You Mean by Building Relationships?

The phrase "building relationships" can sometimes conjure up visions of touchy-feely love-fests. In the context of the kind of classroom this book will be describing, nothing could be further from the truth.

There can be a tendency in our society to focus on accomplishing the task to the detriment of developing relationships. Community organizers try to place the relationship as the priority and, as a result, tend to find that tasks get accomplished more effectively. Doing the same in schools can create a better environment for educators to challenge students (and themselves) to move outside comfort zones (in a *stimulating* and not a *stressful* way) (see Figure 1.1).

Applying an intentional relationship-building practice in the classroom can contribute toward building a challenging and engaging academic atmosphere. Many students, like most people, enjoy talking about themselves and like it when others are interested in hearing what they have to say. In addition, many students would like to develop more connections with their peers and with their teachers. The examples in this chapter help channel these desires into rigorous language development activities.

IN TASKS	IN RELATIONSHIPS
We talk, they listen.	We have a two-way conversation.
Leads with the mouth.	Leads with the ears.
Takes your energy.	Builds on student energy.
Views students as a jar to be filled-up. Involves selling.	Invites students to think through ideas and concepts. Focuses on drawing out.
Can use manipulation, cajoling, tricks.	Uses values and self-interests to tap intrinsic motivation.
Tends to look at short-term results.	Tends to look at long-term results.
Might work in your classroom.	Tends to work in your classroom and beyond.

Figure 1.1 Chart showing the differences between "task" and "relationships."
This chart is modified from one developed by Mike Miller of the Organize Training Center in San Francisco ("Task versus Relationship," Organize Training Center, April, 1985, used with permission of the author).

The relationships built and the information learned about the student's self-interests can be used to stimulate students to deepen engagement in language learning. One way to do this is by framing the work in the context of their self-interests—their visions for themselves, what they want to learn, and how they want to learn it. Having a trusting relationship increases the likelihood that people will share their true self-interests and not just the ones they think the teacher and other students wants to hear. It's about *probing* (defined in the dictionary as "to search thoroughly") and not *prodding* (defined as "to poke with a stick" or "to goad"). Teachers can then frame propositions or invitations for action in the context of students' self-interests and help them tap into their own intrinsic motivation.

Classroom Story

Students are generally aware of their self-interests but sometimes may need to be reminded or helped to clarify them. One of my students was feeling less than enthusiastic about completing an in-class writing assignment. I was being gently supportive, but it was clear he was getting ready to give up. I asked him, "Isaac, you've told me in the past that you wanted to be a carpenter and run your own business. Is that still what you hope to do?" He responded that he wanted to pursue that dream. I went on, "I know you can do it. If you really want to, though, you're going to need to fill out building permits and other government forms. How are you going to be able to do that if you can't write well in English?" I went on to tell him that as long as he told me that was the career he wanted, I would push him on developing the skills he would need to accomplish it. Ultimately, I told him, it was his choice to make—I wasn't going to nag him. Another old organizing adage is if you don't give people the opportunity to say no, you don't give them the opportunity to say yes, either. Without people having that power, they tend not to own their response.

Isaac decided to try his best on the writing assignment. Most importantly, it was *his* decision to do so—*his* energy. In a relationship-oriented classroom, the energy tends to come from students. In a task-oriented classroom, the bulk of the energy tends to come from the teacher. Could I have tried to control the situation by just telling him to get back to work, and telling him he would get an "F" if he didn't complete it? Sure. Would he have done it? Yes, he probably would have at least gone through the motions of doing so. Of course, it would have been my energy moving it forward, it is unlikely to have been his best work, and it certainly would not have helped him develop any sense of intrinsic motivation.

Of course, it was possible that he would have responded to my question by saying he didn't want to be a carpenter and own a business any longer. What would I have done in that case? First, it's important to use this tactic carefully. Based on my ongoing relationship with Isaac, and our numerous conversations, I knew he was very committed to that vision for himself. However, if he had surprised me by saying no, I might have asked him if he could really think of a career he might want to do where writing was not going to be important. I might have asked him to think about it for a few minutes and had him make a list of other careers he might be interested in. I might then have come back to talk and see if we agreed that he wouldn't need to write in English to be successful in them. And if that didn't work, I might have just asked him to take a break from the assignment, given him several other choices of things to do, and then revisited the issue later that same day or the next.

But the point of developing a relationship is not just to manipulate people to do something you want. The Indo-European roots of the word "relationship" mean to "carry back." A genuine relationship is an exchange. It's not only considering how you can affect the other person, but also being open to see how that other person can affect you. It's sharing parts of your story as well as listening to theirs. My life is richer from learning about Ukrainian culture from Ivana and from what I have learned from others and about myself during these listening efforts.

People may very well risk more in the context of a trusting relationship and in the context of a group of trusting relationships. When community organizing groups get into tense political battles and are attacked in the media and through other avenues, most members do not desert the organizations even though some might be under tremendous pressure to do so. Many often stay less because of the political issue and more because of their commitment to relationships with other members and with the organizers.

There is an old organizing saying that goes like this: A group of people in a room that don't know each other can be a mob. A group of people in a room that are in relationship with one another is power. The same holds true for a classroom.

What Does Research Say about Building Relationships in the Classroom?

There is a great deal of research documenting the importance of relationship building in the classroom to promote student achievement, particularly with English language learners.

This section will focus on three elements of this research:

✦ How teacher–student and peer relationships create a classroom climate, and its effect on English language learners.

✦ The critical importance of using schema, or students' previous experience, in helping English language learners understand new concepts.

✦ The effect self-interest has on student motivation, especially on English language learners.

When considering the last two points, it's important to remember what was discussed earlier in this chapter—it's difficult to learn what has been important in a person's life, and their hopes and dreams, without having a genuine relationship.

Relationships and Classroom Climate

Studies have documented the effect that positive relationships in school have on students. The Search Institute is a national organization that has developed a list of positive assets students need in order to succeed based on research and a survey of 2 million students between the grades of 6 and 12. They have found that

> young people who said they had 'caring and fair staff' at their school were much more likely to also feel confident about their ability to succeed academically—73% had academic confidence—than were students who didn't see their staff as caring and fair, only 47% of whom had academic confidence. (Starkman, Roberts, and Scales 5)

Developing self-confidence, of course, is essential in learning a second language.

In a review of 4,000 studies and articles on cooperative learning involving students between grades six and nine in 2006, the Cooperative Learning Institute computed the impact that relationships had on student achievement. They found that "over 3/4's of the variation in academic achievement was explained by the quality of interpersonal relationships." The study went on to say that "a teacher's secret strategy for increasing student achievement may be building more positive relationships among students" (Johnson, Johnson, and Roseth 3).

Dr. Jami Jones highlights research that documents the importance of relationships in developing teen resiliency (the ability to persevere and adapt in the face of challenges). Jones cites research done by Emmy E. Werner and Ruth Smith, who list "making connections and being mentored" and "social skills" as two important factors in teen resiliency.

Robert J. Marzano, the well-known and respected education researcher, also emphasizes the importance of relationships in the classroom. "If the relationship between the teacher and the students is good," he writes, "then everything else that occurs in the classroom seems to be enhanced" (Marzano 150). A 2009 study on the importance of relationships in student success had similar findings (Bergin and Bergin 1).

A recent major study focusing on how supportive relationships affect the school life of immigrant youth emphasizes the significance of such relationships for English language learners. After following over 400 recently arrived youth over a five-year period, Carola Suarez-Orozco, Allyson Pimentel, and Margary Martin concluded that these kinds of relationships are particularly critical for English language learners so they can develop feelings of safety and see possibilities of academic success (Suarez-Orozco, Pimentel, and Martin 15).

Research on learning and the brain highlights why the development of a supportive web of classroom relationships is critical for the English language learner. The brain goes into survival mode when it feels threatened. Eric Jensen, a pioneer in brain-based research, has found that when students feel threatened (for example, through potential embarrassment) "the brain is put on alert, defense mechanisms and behaviors are activated, which is great for survival, but not good for learning" (Jensen 237). When the brain is feeling threatened, higher-order thinking skills are impaired.

Stephen Krashen makes another point specifically for English language learners. He writes, "The best [second-language teaching] methods are therefore those that supply 'comprehensible input' in low-anxiety situations, containing messages that students really want to hear" (Krashen, *Principles and Practice* 6).

A safe environment for English language learners is one where they feel confident to take risks. Placing a priority on building relationships is one strategy to help create that kind of atmosphere.

Research in Action

At the beginning of each school year, and now and then throughout the subsequent months, one potential way to reinforce this kind of classroom culture is by leading a discussion on the differences between a classroom of students and a community of learners. The Latin and Indo-European root words for "community" mean an "exchange shared by all." Without this kind of community, we instead create a "class" or a "classroom," which is defined in many dictionaries as just "a group of students meeting together to be taught."

One topic to cover might be how classes respond to student mistakes. Students might say that typically in their classes (if, of course, they've ever been in school before) those who make mistakes are ridiculed. The educator could then explain how in a community of learners, those students are supported for taking risks. Students could then decide what kind of culture they would prefer, why, and what the educator and students have to do together to create it.

Using Schema

Schema is the background knowledge that we bring to learning a new concept, text, or situation. It is the lens through which we see and interpret something that is new to us.

English language learners often have very different background knowledge than what native speakers bring to class. By learning about students' lives, educators can more effectively connect those experiences with new classroom content (Alliance for Excellent Education 2). In other words, developing relationships helps teachers gain an understanding of students' background knowledge that they can then relate to academic content.

Research in Action

A class of predominantly Hmong students was learning a Native American folktale from the Iroquois people. Their teacher was able to use the knowledge gained through conversations with students about the several major Hmong clans, and the oppression the Hmong had experienced by the Chinese and then other Laotians as they were expelled from their homes, to very quickly help them gain a basic understanding of Native Americans and their history.

Brain-based research also demonstrates that whenever something new "is presented in such a way that students see relationships [with existing knowledge], they generate greater brain cell activity and achieve more successful long-term memory storage and retrieval" (Willis 15).

There will be more about the importance of schema in the next chapter, "Accessing Prior Knowledge through Stories."

Student Self-Interest

Research shows that in order for effective learning to take place, students have to feel that what is being taught is relevant to their needs.

Writers and researchers ranging from Stephen Krashen (*Principles and Practice* 66), William Glasser (21), and researchers who have applied Lev Vygotsy's theories to second language learning (Lantolf and Appel 212) have confirmed this conclusion. No matter how many different creative tactics an educator might employ in his or her classroom, many students will not be engaged in learning unless they perceive the content to be helpful to their lives. Whether these are immediate and short-term goals or longer-term hopes for the future, it is difficult for educators to know what these needs truly are without having a relationship where students feel comfortable sharing them.

Of course, sometimes people are not necessarily clear on their self-interests and need some agitation to help clarify them. A student might not initially see a reason to learn about how the U.S. legislative process works. However, if you know from engaging with the student that he misses his grandfather in Mexico, you might explain the lesson in the context of why or why not an immigration reform bill will pass Congress, and the impact that bill will have on whether his grandfather would be permitted to join his family in the United States.

One of the best ways to teach English is to first find out what content students really want to learn, and then have them use English to learn it.

What Are Examples of Building Relationships in the Classroom?

It's important to recognize that building and maintaining relationships happens over time, and self-interests continually change. Many of the classroom activities shared in this chapter can happen at the beginning of the school year *and* on a regular basis during the entire school year.

There are various specific projects related to building relationships that students can create during the course of a year. For example, they could do one project each quarter, including an oral presentation, which would be coordinated with regular individual assessments. These presentations provide an opportunity to create follow-up individual conversations (since strong relationships are generally built on a one-to-one basis) and maximize the potential for their success. In addition, these student projects are ways that students can also develop their writing, speaking, listening, and reading skills.

The introductions lesson plan is for one of these projects. Others listed in this section can follow similar steps.

Introductions Lesson Plan

Instructional Objectives

Students will:

1. Learn to write grammatically correct sentences, including questions.

2. Learn and practice public and one-on-one speaking skills.

3. Learn and practice listening skills.

4. Learn new vocabulary.

5. Demonstrate their reading fluency.

Duration

Three 55-minute class periods for teacher modeling, student preparation, and student practice (this could be reduced to two days if necessary).

Fifteen minutes at the beginning of the following class and 15 minutes at the end of class for five additional days of student presentations.

English Language Development Standards
California English Language Development (ELD) Domains

1. Students use English for everyday communication in socially and culturally appropriate ways and apply listening and speaking skills and strategies in the classroom.

2. Students will apply the conventions of standard English usage orally and in writing.

Materials

1. One copy for each student of a sentence-starter sheet saying:

Who am I?

My name is _____.

My loves: I love _____ because _____.

My joys: I feel joy when I _____ because _____.

My worries: I worry about _____ because _____.

My sadnesses: I feel sad when _____ because _____.

My hopes and dreams: I hope _____ because _____.

2. Poster sheets at least 11" $\times$ 14" for each student

3. Colored markers

4. Old magazines, scissors, and glue (optional)

5. Teacher-prepared model poster

6. One copy for each student of a question-starter sheet saying:

What is your favorite _____?

Can you tell me about a time you _____?

Who is your favorite _____?

7. Simple public speaking rubric listing a few key elements:

Did I try my best on the poster?

Did I look at the audience while I spoke?

Did I speak loudly and clearly?

Procedure

First Day

1. Teacher explains that one way we can get to know each other better and practice our English skills is by introducing ourselves. As part of that the class is going to first review the meaning of some words. The words *love, joy, worry, sad, hope,* and *dream* are written on the board. Students are asked to write the words down and write or draw a picture as a definition of each word if they can; they are told it's okay if they guess or don't know. After

students finish, they are divided into groups of three for five minutes to share their definitions with their group. Teacher circulates and identifies students who have particularly good images or word definitions and asks them to be prepared to share with the class. Teacher ends small groups and calls on those students to share with the whole class. (If time is an issue, this whole section could be eliminated and teacher could just review vocabulary terms with students and start poster preparation during the second half of this class).

2. Teacher distributes the sentence-starter sheet and reviews it with the class. She explains that she will do it first.

3. Teacher then presents her poster.

4. Teacher asks class what she did well in the presentation and highlights certain techniques (letters in poster are clearly written, look at the audience, speak clearly and loudly, not chewing gum).

5. Teacher explains that students will have one full class period to prepare their posters, and part of a class period to practice. Teacher assigns a student schedule for presentations.

Second Day

1. Teacher reviews sentence-starter sheet and leaves her poster on the board as a model. She explains as students are working on their posters that she will call them over to her individually to have them read to her for a minute. She explains it is not a test and is just a way for her to become a better teacher for them. She distributes posters and markers (and magazines, scissors, and glue if she decides to use them). Students have whole class period to work on their own poster.

2. While students are working on posters, teacher has individual students read a simple passage at the appropriate reading level. Without obviously watching the time, she records how many words are read accurately in one minute (mispronounced words are not included). More importantly, this brief time is used by the teacher to learn a little more about the student by asking questions.

Third Day

1. Students are divided into groups of three and practice their poster presentations for 20 minutes. Teacher explains that each student should be prepared to say one thing they liked about the others' presentations and one thing that they think could be improved. Teacher models some examples.

2. Teacher distributes and reviews question-starter sheet, and explains that students will be given a chance to ask questions of each student speaker. She reviews her poster and models some potential questions based on it.

3. Teacher asks students to think about what a good listener does, then write it down, and then share with a partner. Teacher circulates and asks particular students to share, and reviews expectations of a good listener: watching the speaker, not making noise, writing good questions down (if time is an issue, this part could be eliminated, and teacher could just review expectations).

Fourth, Fifth, Sixth, Seventh, and Eighth Day

1. Students make their presentations during the first and last 15 minutes of class. After each presentation, teacher encourages at least one question to be asked and calls on individual

students to share what they thought the presenter did well and what they could have done better. In addition, each student completes a rubric grading themselves after their presentation.

Assessment

Students and teacher uses simple public speaking rubric listed earlier. If desired, teacher can develop a similar rubric for students to assess their listening skills.

Possible Extensions/Modifications

Students in the preproduction stage of language acquisition can show their poster without speaking.

In the lesson plan, note the importance of teacher modeling, small groups, and presentation logistics—there is nothing deadlier than 20 or 30 consecutive presentations over a day or two, so it's best to schedule 2 or 3 at the beginning and 2 or 3 at the end of each class over four or five days. Individual assessments are less about gathering data and more about spending a few minutes with each student to have a conversation. One student at a time can come to the teacher's desk to check in (How are things going your classes? What do you like most about school? How are your brothers and sisters?) for several minutes, and then they can spend one minute reading orally.

Student–student relationship building can continue with 10-minute one-on-one conversations that each student can have with every other student in the class over a period of weeks following all the presentations. Two of these individual meetings can happen each day—one at the beginning of class and one at the end.

The sheet shared in the lesson plan of question starters that don't necessarily lead to yes-or-no answers (though, of course, depending on the English level of students there might be some of those, too) can help students prepare for these individual meetings. Educators can also model an individual conversation with students before they begin doing them, and they will also have had their experience of a similar conversation during the individual assessments. It's important to highlight that it's not just a question and answer session and that students can share unsolicited thoughts.

Here are some examples of what students have written under the categories in their "Who am I?" posters. There is certainly an enormous amount of grist in them to be used in individual conversations (potential follow-up questions are in parentheses):

My Loves: I Love . . .

Thailand (What do you love about Thailand? Why did your family leave?)

My family (How many brothers and sisters do you have? Are you the oldest? Youngest?)

Soccer (What position do you play? What other sports do you play?)

My Joys: I Feel Joy When . . .

I sing (What do you like to sing?)

I'm with my girlfriend (Can you tell me about her?)

When I go shopping (Where do you like to go shopping? What do you like to buy?)

My Worries: I Worry About . . .

Not passing the high school exit exam (What is the hardest part for you? Why?)

My sister (Why?)

My English (What is the hardest about learning English for you?)

My Sadnesses: I Feel Sad When . . .

I have homework (What class gives you most homework? What is the hardest?)

My dog died (What kind of dog was it? What did it look like?)

I can't help myself (What things can't you do?)

My Hopes and Dreams: I Hope That . . .

I will see my dog (What kind of dog is it? Is it lost? What does it look like?)

I will be a newspaper reporter (Why? What do you want to write about?)

I will be a better student (What do you want to do better?)

Additional Student Presentation Projects

Here are some additional student projects that could use very similar lesson plans (All meet the same academic standards listed in the lesson plan):

Complete a series of sentence starters, including "My name is_____. I'm from _____. This is a map of my native country. This is a picture of me. This is a picture of my family. This [an object they bring to school] is important to me because _____. [You can ask students to bring up to five objects.]

Make a collage of pictures from magazines of things they like and/or that represent them, and write a sentence describing what each one is and why it represents them (with sentence starters, again).

Present an "I'm Good At . . ." poster, where they describe the things they're good at, ranging from playing soccer to making tamales to playing video games.

Design a family tree that also includes what people did (and do) as their profession, stories about them, and so forth.

Create a "Life Graph" (Burke 240) where students make a timeline of their life with images and text. In addition, the timeline is in a graph form where student rate how positive or negative each experience was. One modification of this project could be having students extend the timeline and project potential future events in their lives, too.

Draw a map of their neighborhood, including examples (in art and in text) of their experiences at different places (their route to school, a party they attended, etc.) (Burke 245).

Tech Tip—Online Slideshow

Students can take any of the presentation project ideas and make high-tech versions of them—both as a change of pace and as an opportunity for others outside the classroom to view them and leave text or audio comments. Students can take digital pictures with their cell phones or classroom cameras and/or grab images off the Web (see Appendix 1 for information on copyright issues). There are slideshow tools for every English and technology level. There are super-easy sites like Bookr (<http://www.pimpampum.net/bookr/>) and Smile Slideshow (<http://www.colgate.com/ColgateSmile/mashup.srv>) that don't require registration and have photos available that can be used. PhotoPeach (<http://photopeach.com/>) is only very slightly more complicated, and also lets users include quizzes in their creations. Then there are sites that are only a little more complex that let users provide audio narration, like VoiceThread (<http://voicethread.com/#home>), Show Beyond (<http://www.showbeyond.com/show/home>) and Slide Six (<http://slidesix.com/>). Of course, both students and teachers should be acquainted with online safety issues before using the Internet. See Appendix 1 for more information.

Tech Tip—Online Timelines

There are several free Web tools that students can use for creating online timelines of their lives. xTimeline (<http://www.xtimeline.com/index.aspx>) is just one, and others can be found in Appendix 1. Students can either use their own images or grab ones off the Web to illustrate important events. Privacy settings can be used to restrict access.

Writing Projects

Students also can maintain a personal journal that they write on individual sheets of paper that they later put into a binder (instead of an educator having to cart home 30 notebooks) where they write about their lives. One day each week students can write a few sentences and draw about something they did—usually including at least two good things that happened and one not-so-good thing that occurred. They can also write what they could have done differently to have helped make the not-so-good occurrence better. Of course, newcomers might only draw at first, and that works fine, too. Sometimes teachers can ask students to imagine something that they would have liked to have done, but did not do. Depending on the English level of the class, teacher-provided sentence starters can help students begin their journal writing (see Figures 1.2 and 1.3).

Students can share these journal entries with their peers orally (as well as showing their pictures) as another relationship-building activity, and they provide the educator with helpful information for use in personal conversations with students (and their parents, if and when educators go on home visits with an interpreter, if necessary). These journals are also important tools to assess student writing progress and to identify common challenges.

Whether it's family members who are ill, parties, feeling angry about something, or concerns about doing something for the first time, there are plenty of things that students will find in common no matter what country they're from or language they speak. And students are developing their English skills at the same time as they are strengthening relationships.

Students can write a version of a dialogue journal. Typically, these are letters that might be written back and forth between teachers and their students. In these letters, instead of

I went to my cousin house, and they did a shamah thing for their family. They kill two pigs and we helped then prepare the ceremony and later we help then clean up. Alco I want then to have a good life in the future.

Figure 1.2 Student journal example showing what they did during the week.

I went to visit my aunt and my cousin in thailand because they are inportant to me. They lived in a good place to safe themself. They have to work on them self and they don't money. but, they have to live nearest at the forest they can find fruit and crops to eat. Most the time they planted some crops. but when it summer time they planted some crops it not grows then they have to go to the forest and find some food to eat that time when that time pass and the crops can grows up than they get amore food to eat every year.

Figure 1.3   Student journal example showing what they *wanted* to do.

educators critiquing incorrect grammar, in the context of their response they instead model the correct form. For example, a student might write, "Yesterday, I help mi muther cook." An educator could then respond, "That's neat that you helped your mother cook yesterday. When I was your age, I helped my mother cook, too."

In one adaptation of these types of journals, students write these letters to pen pals in a class of native speakers in the same school. Not only do these letters create opportunities for relationship building with students outside of English language learner classes (this type of sister class relationship can also include periodic face-to-face meetings), but the teacher in the more advanced sister class can use it to help her/his students develop better grammar skills, as well. It fits in with the adage you never really learn something until you have to teach it. A similar project can be useful in a mixed-class of native speakers and English language learners.

All this student writing, in addition to helping facilitate relationship building, also provides an enormous amount of material to use to teach vocabulary, reading strategies, and grammar. More specific examples of how to do this will be included in chapter 4, "Learning by Doing." The student projects in this section correlate with California ELD domains 5 and 6.

Tech Tip—Writing Online

If a computer is available, having students either write their journals in a word processing document or on a blog is an option. The automatic grammar and spell-check features available in most software can be particularly helpful to English language learners, though it might be best to have students write initial drafts in by hand so that the corrections do not inhibit their writing. According to a study of Maine's ambitious program of giving a computer to every middle-school student, improved writing has been the major measurable academic benefit. One of the study's authors says that computers "make it easier for students to edit their copy and make changes without getting writer's cramp. . . . As a result, students are writing and revising their work more frequently, which leads to better results. And it's important . . . that those skills translated when the test was taken with pen and paper, too" (eSchool News 1). Writing in a blog has also been shown to be particularly helpful to English language learners (Fellner and Apple 15). The possible use of blogs for cooperative projects with classes in other parts of the country and/or world will also be explored further in chapter 4, "Learning by Doing." Details on blogs can be found in Appendix 1.

Games

Doing class work through cooperative learning groups and dividing the class into small groups to compete in learning games are other ways to help build relationships and reinforce what is being studied at the same time. (You can find a list of simple games requiring little equipment or preparation in Appendix 2.) The educator can choose the teams (at least for the first part of the year) to ensure that students are not staying with the same students all the time and that there's a mixed ethnic and English competency level in each one. The student projects in this section correlate with California ELD domain 1.

Connecting to Student Self-Interests

It's obviously not feasible to work on everyone's immediate self-interests at the same time. We may be covering subjects at times which, for some of our students, might be a stretch for them to see how it's relevant to their lives. We can help them to see how it is. At the same time, through our relationships with them, we can also find other ways that connect to their broader self-interests. These could include a desire to work on projects together with other students even if they are less than enthralled with the project itself. Playing games, demonstrating with pride to their family about a job well done, or just satisfying a hunger to learn new things might be other self-interests felt by our students, and it's incumbent on us as teachers to learn what they are. Good teaching is a process of drawing out and not just filling up.

Reading Projects

The examples shared in this chapter so far demonstrate students using the concept of relationship-building and self-interest to also strengthen writing, speaking, and listening skills. These same concepts can enhance reading.

One way that was mentioned earlier in the chapter to introduce the importance of developing a supportive classroom atmosphere was by contrasting how a community of learners would respond to people making mistakes differently than would a classroom of students. Another way to reinforce the importance of relationships is by having students read some very short stories connected to the concept. In addition, these stories are opportunities for students to: develop word analysis skills, vocabulary knowledge, and reading fluency by making them into clozes (fill-in-the-blank), asking for students to identify and categorize words, and practice reading the stories in pairs. Students can also apply various other reading strategies depending on their English level, including sharing if and how they can make a personal connection ("This reminds me of when . . .") to the story.

School librarians might be particularly helpful in identifying written stories (both from student cultures and from others) and videos that emphasize the concept of relationship building.

Various stories can be used as templates and changed to reflect student ethnicity, background knowledge, and English level. One template is a story about Martin Luther King, Jr. that comes from the book *Parting the Waters* by Taylor Branch:

> While many previous pastors at his [Martin Luther King, Jr.'s] first church always asked members "*What* are you doing?" King always asked everyone *how* they were doing, usually following with a personal question about their health or the kids. Moreover, he would linger over such conversations against all competing obligations. (Branch 119)

In addition to the reading skills and strategies students use with this story, discussion questions can include: "Would you like this person? Why or why not?" and "Have you ever known anyone like him/her (depending on which gender used in that particular version of the story)? If so, who was he/she and what did he/she do?"

The student projects in this section correlate with California ELD domains 2, 3, 4, and 6.

How Can Technology Be Used to Develop and Deepen Face-to-Face Relationships?

Stephen Krashen, in "Free Voluntary Reading," has documented how having students read books of their choice can be an extraordinarily effective method of language acquisition. It certainly fits into the idea of making classroom content relevant to students' lives—most will see reading what they want to as being in their self-interest. Krashen's theory of free voluntary reading (it's also called pleasure reading) can be implemented particularly effectively through the use of computers, and at the same time technology can be used to deepen face-to-face relationships.

How do you implement Krashen's theory of free voluntary reading (letting students choose to read what they want) when you are teaching classes of preliterate high school Hmong students who have just arrived from Thailand?

That was one of a number of questions facing Luther Burbank High School in Sacramento when many Hmong teenagers—part of a group of 2,000 Hmong refugees—arrived in the area in 2005.

The Hmong are an ethnic group from Laos that provided tens of thousands of soldiers to the CIA during the Vietnam War. The U.S. government had promised that, if they lost the war, they would bring the Hmong to the United States. Thousands have come over the years, and one of the last Hmong refugee camps in Thailand, housing 10,000 people, was closed in 2005. California's Central Valley and St. Paul, Minnesota have the largest concentrations of Hmong residents. Since this last resettlement program was based on family connections, many of these final refugees arrived in these same two areas.

Few of the new students had ever attended school before. Even fewer others in their families had, either. It was indeed a great opportunity. How often can high school educators say that their class is the first experience of school for their students?

As educators began to help students learn English and become acclimated to their new country, they began to think more and more about how to implement free voluntary reading. It was a key component of many of the mainstream English classes at the school, and it certainly fit in with the organizing philosophy of assisting people to freely choose and act on their own behalf. Burbank didn't have tutors who could work individually with each student, so they needed to find another way.

Teachers decided to explore how they could take advantage of computer technology to help implement free voluntary reading with their students *and* develop strategies to use the same technology to help students develop and deepen face-to-face relationships.

The school created a Web page (<http://larryferlazzo.com/english.html>) with links to a few of these free sites, and opened a before- and after-school computer lab for Hmong and other English language learner students. Within two weeks over 100 students were coming each day, plus 15 bilingual students who offered to volunteer as peer tutors. Students were provided headphones and were able to access any of growing number of links on the Web site (it now has over 9,000 links that are specifically accessible to English language learners related to all academic subjects). In addition to just engaging with the computer screen, students would discuss in class what they were reading and make recommendations to each other.

Though the students attending were predominantly Hmong, a growing number of recent immigrant students from other countries began attending the lab (over half of the school's student population is composed of English language learners). In another initial effort to use computers to build face-to-face relationships, students would regularly be paired with someone who spoke a different native language to introduce themselves and compete with each other in their favorite online language development games, which can be found both on the Web site and in Appendix 1.

Within four months, students participating in the lab had a 50 percent greater improvement on reading fluency and cloze (fill-in-the-blank) assessments than students in a control group (for more information, see my Web site, <http://larryferlazzo.com/familyliteracy.html>). As a result of teacher home visits, a family literacy project was also begun by providing home computers and Internet access to immigrant families. You can read more about that project in Ferlazzo and Hammond's book *Building Parent Engagement in Schools*.

The school librarian also assisted in this effort by identifying and acquiring paper books on topics that students had identified as being of high interest and that they had discovered on the computer.

The school continues to explore ways to use the Internet to facilitate face-to-face relationships. One way has been to take advantage of Web 2.0 advances to enable students to easily create content that can be posted on the Web and accessed by students and their families. This content can then be shared and time made in class to discuss their creations. By using computers as a tool to promote interpersonal relationships, we can maximize individual achievement in English language development.

The projects shared in this technology section correlate with California ELD domains 1, 5, and 6.

Tech Tip—Using Viral Marketing

The recent craze of viral marketing—which includes companies creating video clips, games, cartoons, and other applications that computer users can modify to send to friends—are a boon to ELL classes. Many of these free tools have text-to-speech or easy audio recording features. Students have created talking cartoon scrambled eggs to discuss what they eat for breakfast and singing e-cards describing how they spend their holidays. Sharing these creations can be excellent relationship-building activities. You can find links to these sites, descriptions on how to use them, and examples of student work in Appendix 1.

Tech Tip—Online Video Games

Students playing online adventure and puzzle video games that have walkthroughs (step-by-step instructions on how to win) are another example of using computers for group work. Students are paired up at one computer and have to work together to follow the instructions to finish the game. Usually, everyone ends up helping everyone else. Students can also easily use Web 2.0 applications to record screencasts of these walkthroughs (or write and record their own) while they are actually playing the game (again, see Appendix 1 for Web site addresses and details). Very animated—and student initiated—discussions in English can occur regularly during and after these game-playing sessions. In fact, now students can use Web applications that allow them to quickly design video games and write instructions on how to play them. Other students can play their games, write comments about them, and discuss them in class. Again, you can find Web sites and their details in Appendix 1.

Tech Tip—Audio Slideshows

Students can also work in groups to easily create audio slideshows on different topics. Digital cameras can be used to take photos for uploading, or, even easier, most online slideshow applications let you grab images off the Web. Students can create a simple storyboard in class on, for example, introducing themselves. After one class period spent preparing the storyboard (a simple series of boxes on a sheet of paper where students write their commentary and decide what image would go with it), a group of two or three students could use an application like VoiceThread to complete a short 10-slide show highlighting the ethnic culture of each student, what they like to do for fun, their favorite book, and a goal they have for the future. Their creations could be posted on a Web site or blog and shown to the entire class if a computer projector is available. Most of these free Web tools also let users leave comments on other people's slideshows. In an idea explored further in the chapter 4, "Learning by Doing," it could also be accessed by sister classes around the world. Again, see Appendix 1 for more information.

How Do You Assess Relationship Building?

As discussed earlier in this chapter, education researchers and neurologists have convincingly determined that placing a priority on building relationships, and its resulting classroom atmosphere, is an objectively valuable educational strategy that results in increased student academic achievement. Moreover, as mentioned previously, English language learners participating in Luther Burbank High School's use of technology to enhance face-to-face relationships had a 50 percent greater increase in their English literacy over those who were not in the program.

What are some ways to determine if one has been effective in developing these solid and supportive educator–student and student–student relationships?

Here are three simple ways to assess success:

One is seeing if a fair amount of present students like to "hang out" in the classroom before school and during lunch, and if students from previous years like to do the same. If they do, then that's a good indicator that an educator has been successful in developing solid relationships with students.

Another way is by letting students choose members of their small cooperative learning groups periodically (instead of the teacher choosing them) to see if they mix them up, or if they always choose the same group members. If they are mixed, that, too, is a fair measure that students have done a good job of developing relationships with other students in class and that there's a greater sense of solidarity among them.

Finally, two or three times a year an anonymous, in-class survey can be distributed. It's actually a two-part survey (done on two separate days)—one focusing on relationships with the educator, and the other on student–student relationships. Figure 1.4 contains a reproducible survey form

Classroom Story—Student Survey

This section will contain the questions and a sample of answers written by students in the author's class, along with a short analysis.

Survey on Student–Teacher Relationship

Do you think Mr. Ferlazzo tries to know you better and cares about what happens in your life? If you think he does, how does he show it? If you think he does not, how does he show he doesn't care?

- ◆ Yes, he ask me question and look at my work.
- ◆ Yes, because sometime I don't understand and he try to help me to understand.
- ◆ Of course he does! He is nice with me and ask me how everything going; school and stuff. He smile and show interest in me.
- ◆ Yes, because when you no come to school he take time explaining what you need to do or ask what happened to you.
- ◆ Yes, I think Mr. Ferlazzo worry about me because when I look sad or something like that he ask me if I am ok.
- ◆ Yes, he make me not a gangster in school.

   Is it important for your teachers to want to know you better and care about what happens to you? Why or why not?

- ◆ Yes, because sometimes people want somebody care about them.
- ◆ Yes, because if they know about me they can help me more.
- ◆ Yes, because I like people caring about each other. I think that's the right thing.
- ◆ Yes, because sometimes I can express with the teacher how I feel if I have some personal problems I can see teacher friend.
- ◆ I think yes because whichever happen in your life affect when you come to school.
- ◆ Yes because they need to understand how I feel.
- ◆ Yes because some students are happy when they come to school but when they at home they are sad and feel sad.

   Does Mr. Ferlazzo listen to your ideas and the ideas of other students in the class? Do you think he cares what you think? How does he show he does care or that he doesn't care?

- ◆ He shows it by asking me "Why I've been absent" or "Why do you so happy today?"
- ◆ Sometimes he listen but I think is hard for him to listen to everybody.

SURVEY ON TEACHER–STUDENT RELATIONSHIPS

1. Do you think your teacher tries to know you better and cares about what happens in your life? If you think he does, how does he show it? If you think he does not, how does he show he doesn't care?

2. Is it important for your teachers to want to know you better and care about what happens to you? Why or why not?

3. Does your teacher listen to your ideas and the ideas of other students in the class? Do you think he cares what you think? How does he show he does care or that he doesn't care?

4. Have you tried to get to know your teacher? If so, how have you tried? If not, why haven't you tried?

SURVEY ON STUDENT–STUDENT RELATIONSHIPS

1. Have you gotten to know other students in the class better this year (semester)? If you think you have, what have you done in class that has helped you get to know them better?

2. Is it important to get to know other students better? Why or why not?

3. What more could we do in class to help you get to know other students better?

4. Did you learn anything from other students in class this year (semester)? What?

Figure 1.4   Student survey form for evaluating relationships.
From English Language Learners: Teaching Strategies that Work by Larry Ferlazzo. Santa Barbara, CA: Linworth. Copyright © 2010.

♦ I think he care what I think and he show me to solve my problem.

♦ Yes, he listen to everybody in class because he want to know students ideas.

♦ Yes. When he listen to me and say: Oh, that's a good idea or something like that. He is respectful.

♦ Yes, but sometimes he don't listen because he is so busy.

♦ Yes, but sometimes he just listen but not take it to heart.

♦ He try to talk to me and ask do I have any problem at home.

♦ Yes, he pay attention when I speak and have some question.

What more could Mr. Ferlazzo do to show he cares about you?

♦ Give me some money.

♦ When he see me like sad he ask me if there something he can help.

♦ Maybe he can give us little prizes for our effort so we are motivated and we want to do more.

Have you tried to get to know Mr. Ferlazzo? If so, how have you tried? If not, why haven't you tried?

♦ I have tried to know Mr. Ferlazzo when I asked him how old are he on his birthday.

♦ No, because there are so many students in this class, and he don't have enough time to let me try to get to know him.

♦ Yes because I try to talk to him more and more.

♦ I don't think so because I'm scare because I cannot speak English.

♦ No, because he is so grumpy.

♦ Yes, I've asked him about his life, how he is, what does he like to do.

♦ I don't want to try because he is teacher, me is student and I don't want to try to know him.

♦ Yes, I try to talk to him more because he is friendly to us.

From these survey results, I would say that students feel like it is important to them that their teachers truly care about what happen in their lives, and not just about what happens in the classroom. It also appears that most students feel that I do care about them.

I think the responses to the question about if I listen to students are very insightful. It seems like I do an okay job of it, but could be a little more present to students and be less preoccupied with doing tasks.

Finally, the issue of being preoccupied with tasks comes up again in the final question. It sounds like I could work on being a little more approachable. Three or four students actually used the word "grumpy," which we had learned in a lesson right before they completed the surveys.

These results also reflect my own self-assessment of my work during that semester. It also points to the importance of not waiting until the end of the school year to do this kind of evaluation. I was able to take these comments to heart at the end of the first semester, and it was clear that students felt more positive about my listening skills and approachability by the time June came around.

Here are the questions, and representative answers, about the quality of relationships among students during a recent year:

Survey on Student–Student Relationships

Have you gotten to know other students in the class better this year (semester)? If you think you have, what have you done in class that has helped you get to know them better?

✦ I know them from doing small group.

✦ Yes, I know other students because they have helped me.

✦ Yes, I know other students in this class. Sometime I don't understand I can ask if they can help me read better.

✦ Yes a little bit. Some of them switched seats and that makes me talk with them. Also work in groups.

✦ Yes, because I come to this class and students interview each other and have a conversation.

✦ Yes, we work in a group, then we share our ideas how to present our presentation. We talked to each other.

✦ I know other people because we share reading.

Is it important to get to know other students better? Why or why not?

✦ Yes, I know other students because the students help me and me have more friends.

✦ Yes, because they are my good friends.

✦ Yes, because in that way we can work better and maybe get friends.

✦ Yes, if we know each other we can help each other.

✦ Yes, because we learn from each other.

✦ Yes, it's very important to know other students because we can learn about their cultures and know who they are.

✦ Yes, it is important because I can help them to do something they do not know how to do.

What more could we do in class to help you get to know other students better?

✦ We have to talk to other students more.

✦ More activities to help each other.

✦ Yes, reading and talking to each other.

✦ Maybe let us chat but without working.

Did you learn anything from other students in class this year (semester)? What?

✦ No, I did not learn anything new from my friends.

✦ I learn about new word and the word I don't know how to read.

✦ Yes, I learn nice word.

✦ Yes they help me learn about the geography.

✦ Yes, I learn some Spanish and Hmong words.

✦ Yes, that I have to respect their ideas because I'm not always right. Also that I have to be patient because we don't work as the same time. Everyone is different.

- ✦ I learned that students don't like to do the same things.
- ✦ Yes, I learned about Mexican and Chinese food.
- ✦ Yes, I learn how to deal with different people.
- ✦ Yes, they have some idea that different from me.

Clearly, a good sense of community was developed during the school year evaluated here, and students saw value and benefit in it. A focus on building relationships provided an enriching experience during that period of time. Even more importantly, based on the comments that many students wrote, one can hope that they now value it enough to initiate more relationship-building activities on their own in their future classes and in other aspects of their life.

What Are the Challenges to Making Building Relationships a Priority in the Classroom?

What are some challenges to educators implementing relationship building, along with the other elements of the organizing cycle, in their classroom?

The major challenges tend to fall into three categories:

- ✦ Developing a clear vision of and commitment to how you might want to integrate the organizing cycle into your teaching strategy
- ✦ Making the time to do it
- ✦ Demonstrating to administrators and other teachers that it is pedagogically sound and connects to state standards

Developing a Clear Vision

A man went by a construction site and encountered a bricklayer working. The man asked him what he was doing. The bricklayer replied, "I'm making bricks." The man walked a few feet further and came upon another bricklayer. He asked him the same question. The bricklayer answered, "I'm making a wall." He then walked by another bricklayer and once again asked the same question. This worker replied, "I'm building a cathedral."

Without careful and strategic planning, we can tend to teach lessons that make bricks and walls instead of cathedrals. We can get caught up in the task of covering the curriculum and lose sight of the fact that spending time on building relationships actually helps our students learn the curriculum better.

This kind of thoughtful planning is the first step in re-imagining our classrooms and our work. Then, as Peter Drucker, the well-known writer on organizational and business development wrote, "The best plan is only . . . good intentions unless it degenerates into work" (Drucker, *Management* 128).

Or, if you prefer a more pithy commentary, there is supposedly an old Chinese proverb: "A person has to stand still for a long time with their mouth open before a roast duck will fly into it."

How do we create time in our busy lives to make these plans and visions a reality?

Making Time

It's important to not do something new without giving up something old—it's challenging, and unpleasant, to try to squeeze blood from a stone as we continue to add things that we want to do to an already full plate.

Prioritizing relationship building in the classroom doesn't really take up much class time to implement. The time it does take generally comes in the form of thinking, planning, and preparing outside of class. Given that, let's look at a general time management framework developed by the Industrial Areas Foundation called *opportunities* and *operations*.

Opportunities are the things that give us the most energy. These occasions might be reading a book, talking to a colleague about some new ideas, reflecting on successes and mistakes, or taking a risk and trying something different. *Operations* are the things that drain us of energy. These are things we should do, have to do, or are expected to do.

Peter Drucker uses a similar framework by distinguishing between "the ability to do things right" and the "ability to get the right things done." He's also referred to the division as "efficiency" versus "effectiveness" (Drucker, *The Effective Executive* 2).

We don't have opportunities all the time. But many operations are just not worth doing, or not worth doing well.

One operation to consider reducing is correcting grammar errors on papers. Much research has shown, as Stephen Krashen concluded in his review of the literature, "Applying the Comprehension Hypothesis," that this kind of error correction has a minimal effect on acquiring language.

John Truscott has also been influential with his contribution to this research. After reviewing the available research, and conducting his own, he, too, concludes that typical grammar error correction (writing notes on students' papers and returning them) is not only ineffective but potentially harmful. He cites many comparative studies that show little or no difference between groups of students who have been in classes where errors have been corrected and other groups where they have not been corrected. In fact, some studies have demonstrated the error correction groups as having lower assessments. He finds that even though error correction might make sense intuitively, it does not fit well into how the complicated process of language acquisition operates. In addition, he writes that this kind of grammar error correction contributes toward stress that further inhibits language learning.

However, that does not mean an educator should not spend time on grammar error correction. It does suggest one should spend less time writing on students' papers, and should, instead, use other strategies including, but not limited to: teaching inductively and the instructional method called "concept attainment" to help students self-correct their errors (these two methods are discussed in the "Learning By Doing" chapter), teacher modeling, the dialogue journals discussed earlier in this chapter, games described in Appendix 2, and other ways.

One other way to create more time for our opportunities is to recognize what might be an operation for us could be an opportunity for someone else. What are the tasks that make up our to-do lists?

Perhaps an educator could become less invested in making sure that *his* classroom or school library looks exactly the way he wants it to look. Instead, educators could work with students to try to make it *his and their* classroom (or school library). This means that students are involved in deciding what furniture and what books go where, how the desks are arranged, and what goes up on the wall. And because it is *their* classroom or library, too, many students could have housekeeping responsibilities that might take them a minute every other day and all spend a few minutes together once each week tidying up the room. Most students can find a task they enjoy doing, whether it's neatening up the nonfiction books or vacuuming the rug. And many students might like a frenzied five minutes spent each Friday cleaning things up. Students don't have to be required to do it, but it might be surprising how few choose not to do the work.

This is an example of turning what is an *operation* for an educator into an *opportunity* for students. As a result, educators spend less time cleaning the room outside of class time, students find a task they enjoy (and book cleaners and dusters get to become more familiar with books they might like), and cleaning time on Friday is yet another experience of relationship building.

Finally, identifying allies, such as other teachers, school librarians, or administrators who are interested in also moving in the direction of the organizing cycle can help with lesson planning and discussing how to overcome obstacles that arise. The next chapter will also include information on using the Internet to expand these personal learning networks (PLNs).

Talking to Administrators and Other Allies

Change in general is hard. Change in schools can be excruciatingly difficult and painful. We are all typically much more comfortable with how we have been doing things than with trying something new.

It's possible that you might be in a school and district where administrators and many other teachers are open to new ideas and are certainly committed to the importance of relationship building. On the other hand, you might be teaching in an entirely different environment where you need to defend changes you might want to consider making after reading this book. You might be in a situation where you must only use certain supposedly research-tested teaching strategies, provide voluminous daily written lesson plans connected to state standards, and stick to a district-mandated textbook each day.

If you feel you need to talk with your administrator about your wanting to emphasize relationship building (or anything else discussed in this book), first keep in mind that it's important to have a relationship with *her*—make sure you know her personal story, her self-interests, her goals. In your conversations, you might also find these following points useful

Research

Extensive research is cited in every chapter of this book that documents the educational value of each element in the organizing cycle, including prioritizing relationship building in the classroom. There are also many other studies that demonstrate relationship building's contribution toward increasing student achievement.

State Standards

Every suggestion shared in this chapter, and in other parts of this book, is directly connected to typical English language development standards for reading, writing, speaking, and listening. In fact, each idea can be tied to *multiple* specific standards. Obviously, each state has different standards. It should, however, be fairly easy for a teacher to make connections to his or her own state requirements.

Mandated Textbook

Many of the relationship-building activities discussed here really don't take up that much class time, so they shouldn't be seen to be conflicting with a textbook-based curriculum. And most teachers are allowed to supplement their texts with supportive materials and exercises, which could certainly include the ideas in this chapter. Many textbook exercises can easily be adapted for use in cooperative learning groups and in classroom games so you can reinforce a sense of community—there certainly isn't a requirement that all students complete all of the questions entirely on their own. In addition, usually some stories found in a textbook can be used to emphasize the importance of building relationships

Building relationships is not an add-on or an ancillary benefit of doing other things in class. It can be a central goal in working with our students, and it can result in extraordinarily enriching experiences for students and educators alike. One of those positive results can be increased student academic achievement and higher levels of English proficiency.

CHAPTER 2

Accessing Prior Knowledge through Stories

We were studying about the Middle Ages in world history class and did a project called "Did Feudalism End in the Middle Ages?" The textbook we were using stated that there were eight specific elements of feudalism:

Men spent most of their time working in the fields.

Women and children took care of farm animals, washed clothes, and planted vegetable gardens.

Women and men began working before sunrise and stopped after sundown.

Children worked with their parents and did not go to school.

Children grew up believing they would not have a better life when they grew older because they were born poor. If you were born poor, you were probably going to stay poor.

Their homes had one or two rooms.

They didn't own the land they farmed.

The police did whatever the rich people told them to do.

The book went on to flatly declare that feudalism had ended with the Renaissance.

I then gave students the following assignment:

First, review the list of eight elements of feudalism, and write about if you have experienced, or are now experiencing, any of them in your own life. If the answer is yes to any of them, describe how it made or makes you feel, and how did you change the situation if it was in the past or what you think you can do to change it if it's in the present. If the answer is no, just leave it blank.

Second, arrange to speak to a parent, grandparent, or another older relative and ask them the same thing. Third, after you have written the answers to all these questions, write what you think is the answer to this question: *Did feudalism end in the Middle Ages?*

Some incredible stories were told, and though a few believed feudalism might have ended *20* years earlier, most believed much of it still existed. We composed and sent a letter to the authors and the textbook publisher questioning their interpretation of when feudalism ended. It went unanswered, which, in itself, provided additional grist for discussion.

Students told their personal stories and *learned* the individual stories of others in their families. Latino, Vietnamese, Mien, and Russian students then *shared* these stories and found that, though they obviously had many differences, they and their families had many life experiences in common. They began to *interpret* things differently—they were able to use this information and develop a more sophisticated understanding of the situation. They then *acted* on this new knowledge. At the same time, they increased their experience with, knowledge of, and willingness to use the English language.

What Do You Mean by Accessing Prior Knowledge through Stories?

This storytelling and storymaking progression—having people individually learn stories, then share them with others in a group, then follow this by developing a different interpretation of these stories, leading finally to individual and collective action—is a key to community organizing (and to teaching and learning) success.

Often low-income people and many others, including English language learners, are looked at through the lens of *deficits*—they don't speak English, or they don't necessarily have much learning in an academic context, or they don't have much political power, or they have disabilities (the list goes on and on). Instead, good organizers, and good educators, look through the lens of *assets*—the culture, prior knowledge, relationships, and *stories*—that everyone can bring to the table. (It should also be pointed out that people are more likely to share these stories if they have a *relationship* with those who are listening.)

People can develop more self-confidence and a greater sense of self-identity through the sharing of these stories. At the same time, they can find common ground across cultures as they develop a narrative together. This greater confidence and connection helps people become more comfortable taking risks—whether that means trying to speak a second language, challenging a public official to solve a community problem, or, as members of Alcoholics and Narcotics Anonymous have found over the years, confronting an addiction.

There are many community organizing examples that have followed this same process: stories of unemployment that lead to the creation of worker-owned cooperative businesses; stories of difficulties cashing checks leading to getting a bank to open a branch in a low-income neighborhood or to the creation of a credit union; and even individual stories of seniors having to run to cross a street resulting in the increase of red light times.

They all begin with individual private stories that, once shared, offered an opportunity for people to advance the understanding of their experience to another level. They were able to connect their *schema* to the *schema* of others to develop a new interpretation of their situation, resulting in a whole new public story being created.

Paulo Freire, the Brazilian educator and author of *the Pedagogy of the Oppressed,* described this way of working with people (including students) as follows: "there are levels of knowledge about the facts they already know, which unveil other ways of knowing. This is a right that the people have, and I call it the right to know better what they already know" (Horton and Freire 157).

What Does Research Say about Accessing Prior Knowledge through Stories?

Extensive research has been done on the role of stories and past experience in learning, particularly in how our brain organizes memory and learns new information.

Renat Nummela Caine and Geoffrey Caine have described, based on the work of earlier researchers, how the brain has two types of memory systems—*taxon* and *locale* (Caine and Caine 42). Taxon learning consists of lists, basic skills, and habits. Our locale memories, on the other hand, create stories of our life experiences—weaving our taxon memories into a sophisticated sense of meaning. For example, our taxon memories enable us to know how to open the door to our home with a key. Our locale memories, on the other hand, can connect that skill with other experiences so we know what to do if we have lost that key. For an English language learner, a taxon memory might be knowing how to decode the world "help." A locale memory would be having the confidence, knowledge, and experience to use the word at an appropriate time to receive assistance.

Research in Action

Another example of the difference between the two types of memories might be a student from an immigrant farmworker family knowing, with his taxon memory, what fruit was described by the English word "grape." His locale memory, on the other hand, would be able to describe in detail the backbreaking labor involved in picking it off the vine each year. Instead of assuming that the only other new vocabulary that should be taught and learned with "grape" should be the other names of fruit, an educator might consider using that opportunity to help students learn words like "hoe," "hot," "hard," and "pick" so that the student can use those words in a simple sentence or two that has more meaning *to him*.

The Caines write that our schools today focus on taxon learning, which responds more to extrinsic motivation and is resistant to change once learned. Locale learning is more intrinsic and is always changing. The Caines emphasize the importance of teaching skills in the context of our students' stories, which they define as "a sequence of experiences with a meaningful theme" (Caine and Caine 122).

For example, the feudalism story that opened this chapter provided numerous opportunities for students to learn phonics, reading strategies, pronunciation skills, and grammar. *But those lessons took place within the framework of their own stories and the stories of their families.*

Judy Willis, a neurologist who became a teacher, has also written about brain-based learning and its relationship to students' past experiences. She writes that "memories with personal meaning are most likely to become . . . long-term memories available for later retrieval" (Willis 20). Without that personal connection, information will be stored in more remote areas of the brain that are not very accessible. By having our students share stories of their past experiences, and helping them develop new interpretations for those stories, we can help them create those personal meanings.

Jerome Bruner, the noted education professor and author, believes that our brains are naturally designed for organizing our experiences into stories. In fact, his research finds that this need for narrative is key to language acquisition, at least for children (Bruner, *Acts of Meaning* 77). He goes on to cite other studies that demonstrate an increased ability to understand and learn individual elements of language if it's done in the context of a story (Bruner, *Acts of Meaning* 80). In other words, the best time to help students learn about phonics, spelling rules, grammar, and so forth is when they are sharing personal stories and not necessarily when teachers are dividing these topics into separate silos without a common area of interaction.

Finally, in the previous chapter, the importance of reducing stress for the English language learner was discussed. Students, by sharing their personal stories, connecting with each other, and developing empathy, can help create the kind of classroom atmosphere more conducive to language learning.

What Are Examples of Accessing Prior Knowledge through Stories in the Classroom?

The life experiences of English language learners create unique opportunities to help them develop both a deeper understanding of English and of other academic content knowledge. In addition, they can also use their stories to help native English speakers gain different perspectives on this same academic knowledge.

Immigration Unit

In the following unit on immigration, you will see that students were immediately and repeatedly asked to relate their own beliefs and experiences to those of other immigrant groups in history. We really only understand new information by connecting it to the experiences we have had already. As Roger Schank writes: "People need a context to help them relate what they have heard to what they already know. We understand events in terms of events we have already understood" (Schank 15).

The purpose of the unit was to examine the experiences of previous immigrants and then examine similarities and differences with those of the students and their families. Students began by examining the first American Indians who crossed the Bering Strait; the role of the Spanish colonizers and their relationship with the, by that time, Native Americans; the Chinese who came during the Gold Rush; and the Japanese, including their internment during World War II.

Students learned about these historical immigrant groups and responses to problems they faced from readings that the school librarian helped compile (including excerpts from primary sources), movies, and field trips (using scavenger hunt photo assignments with disposable cameras) to Angel Island (the Ellis Island of the west, through which hundreds of thousands of Chinese immigrants entered the United States), Chinatown in San Francisco, and to a local museum's exhibit re-creation of a barracks in a California Japanese-American internment camp. This information included strikes organized by Chinese workers on the railroads and court challenges to Japanese internment camps in World War II. In addition to the content knowledge they learned, countless language development opportunities were also embedded in the activities. Students:

✦ created Venn diagrams comparing and contrasting immigrant experiences;

✦ read, categorized, and prepared data sets (more about these in chapter 4);

✦ created and completed clozes (also known as "fill-in-the-blanks");

✦ responded to short read-alouds accompanied by both literal and interpretative questions;

✦ composed online descriptions of their field trips and traced immigration patterns using mapping applications; and

✦ completed exercises where they were given sections of passages of text that they then had to put in order. They also had to explain their reasons for placing the passages in the sequence they used.

Tech Tip—Online Maps

There are many free online tools—several that don't even require registration—where students can either upload their own images or grab them off the Web, write descriptions, and trace a field trip or an immigration pattern. Each point in the map can have its own image and student-written text, and several tools allow you to virtually draw a line through them tracing the journey. See Appendix 1 for more details.

Students approached reading about these historical experiences by interacting with the text through using various reading strategies. Even beginning English language learners demonstrated the ability to show they could make connections to the text, visualize, ask questions, predict, evaluate (liking or not liking, agreeing or disagreeing), summarize, and monitor and repair their comprehension. Generally, the educator would pass out a short reading and divide students into pairs strategically (making sure students were in mixed groups ethnically and with different English levels). Then, students would take turns reading sentences to each other, and they would demonstrate a different reading strategy for each paragraph, along with underlining words that were "new to them" (better to use that phrase instead of "words you didn't understand" to emphasize a more affirming message). Students would then sometimes share their responses with another pair. The educator might ask particular students to duplicate what they wrote or drew on the overhead (or have them show their work directly on a document camera if available), or the lesson might go directly into a class-wide discussion of the reading.

Tech Tip—Annotating Web Pages

Annotating the text by either writing directly on it or by using Post-its are great ways for students to demonstrate their use of reading strategies. There are several free and easy-to-use Web tools that let students do the same with virtual Post-its while reading online resources. In fact, there are some resources like Blerp (<http://www.blerp.com/browser/index>) that not only let you write virtually on any Web page of your choosing and then save it, but they let you see how other students have annotated it, too. See Appendix 1 for details.

Students knew that, prior to asking for volunteers, the educator would generally call on different students to share first, so everyone needed to be prepared to speak. Because of an idea that the educator had borrowed from the author of the "California Teacher Guy" blog, students knew the phrase "I don't know" was outlawed in class. Instead, it always had to be replaced with "I'm not sure, but I think that . . ." A large sign was located on the classroom wall and acted as a constant reminder. This tactic, which encouraged and supported the characteristic of taking risks—an essential characteristic of an effective second language learner (more about this in chapter 3)—helped ensure an engaged classroom discussion.

These discussions regularly included a transparency of the text on the overhead, simple teacher drawings on the board, bringing students up for role-plays to illustrate concepts and definitions (nothing beats helping students understand the word "uprising" than bringing one up to the front of the class to represent a Spanish colonizer and then have the rest of the class be Native Americans and throw crumpled balls of paper at him), and regularly checking for understanding ("if it's clear now, everyone show me thumbs up; if not, show thumbs-down; and if it's sort of clear show your thumb on the side"—always reminding students at the same time that's okay to not put their thumbs up).

After studying each ethnic group's experience in California history, students prepared projects answering these questions:

Who were they and how did they get here?

What problems did they face?

How did they respond to those problems?

How do you think you would have responded to those problems and why?

Have you or your families ever been in a similar situation and what did you do?

Jee wrote that the Spaniards forced "the Native Americans to change their culture and way of life." He continued, "The Vietnamese treated my grandpa like a slave when they took over Laos . . . My grandpa and other people had to leave Laos and moved to Thailand for better life." Vi Chai shared:

> The North Vietnamese have treated my family unfairly. The Vietnamese forced them to work for them and they also killed them. My family responded to them by doing what the Vietnamese told them to do. They didn't want to do this, but they had to or else they will die. My family were treated like the Native Americans and they both did the same things, too.

Miguel said if he had been in the position of the Native Americans, he would have "gathered a group of people so that I would be strong for our freedom and so that everything would be like before."

Each time the class completed a short study of an ethnic group's immigration experience in California, students converted their responses to the questions into a different form of presentation—

either as a foldable (<http://larryferlazzo.edublogs.org/2009/06/07/the-best-teacher-resources-for-foldables/>) or an online project. These included

✦ a flipbook,

✦ a simple booklet,

✦ a triorama or diorama,

✦ a comic strip, and

✦ an annotated timeline

Tech Tip–Digital Storytelling

Telling stories using online tools such as video editors, comic strip creators, slide-show makers, and timeline applications can provide value-added benefits to students as they use primary source materials available on the Internet, and it can give them an opportunity to write for a more authentic audience (in other words, some-one other than their teacher or classmates). Even if you don't have a sister class elsewhere, there are many sites where students can post their creations and other people from around the world can benefit from seeing their work. Many are listed in Appendix 1. One in particular that works well with English language learners is a tool called File2.ws (<http://file2.ws/>). No registration is necessary, and all that has to be done is upload any document and it immediately becomes a Web page. Students write a little bit, copy and paste some images, and–voila!–they have an online story to share.

Students would then put their desks into two rows facing each other and move to the next per-son every few minutes, or get into small groups, and share their responses to those questions (a similar system was used in the computer lab for online projects). There was always special interest in how they have would have responded and why and if their families had ever faced similar situations. Clearly, student interest was sparked most by relating content to their own lives.

Students were also divided into groups and shared what they had learned with other classes. In an article written for *Education Week*, Debra Viadero has highlighted numerous studies that have shown peer teaching/tutoring to be beneficial to both the tutor and the one being tutored, particularly with inner-city and ethnic minority students. Finally, and most importantly, students periodically reflected on what was discussed in class, considering if they would change anything they wrote based on what they had heard from other students. Many students (both immigrants and nonimmigrants), after having learned directly about what some of the Hmong refugees experienced, weren't as certain as they had been before about what they would have done if they were a Native American dealing with Spaniards. Heroic armed resistance against an overwhelming foe didn't sound as easy after having learned what happened to their class-mates and their families who had tried it. They weren't quite as disdainful of the choice many Native Americans had made to live under the Spaniards instead of being killed. Community organizers call this a "judgment"—a conclusion reached after talking with others—as opposed to an "opinion"—a feeling based only on one's own thoughts.

At least some students recognized that perhaps not all things are as black and white as they might appear. The educator asked students to share instances in their lives when they were *sure* they had been right and others wrong—arguments with their parents or friends, or actions taken by certain politicians. Had they really taken time to consider why that person felt or acted the way he or she did? Students primarily shared stories of home or school tension—wanting to stay out later at night, for example, or being sure that a class assignment was dumb. All confessed that they never thought at the time about the reasons their parents or teachers might have had for their actions.

The point of this classroom experience is not to promote the idea that slavery is something good. Instead, it illustrates that having students develop their own individual stories and then share them with others can help them develop a new and different interpretation of events. This interpretation can lead to action. It led many students to begin to rethink both a historical event and the actions of others. This kind of classroom experience can promote the development of empathy—the ability to genuinely put yourself in another's shoes—a crucial skill in leading a healthy and compassionate life.

Next, the class spent time studying more recent immigration patterns and stories, particularly the ones represented by students in our class—Hmong, Mexican, Russian, and Vietnamese. Using similar methods to those outlined earlier, including read-alouds, data sets, and interacting with the text, the class learned about these immigration sagas. Each student then prepared his or her own family's immigration story, in which he or she was asked to answer a series of questions:

Why did you come here?

Why do you think others stayed in your native country?

What happened during your trip to the United States?

What is your life here like?

What do you miss?

Would you ever go back?

What are your hopes for the future?

They then shared their answers, accompanied by hand-drawn illustrations, in small booklets, with other students in the class.

Ma thought that "some people stayed behind because they believe that American are monsters and will eat them alive, and some leave because they want to see America and better their lives." Nayeli wrote that some people leave her country because "their dreams are bigger than their fears." Jee wrote that he hoped "someday I will become a teacher or a police if I study hard. I would like to be citizen of America."

Sergio wrote that "the life here is fun and good, but I don't like that here is some people dislike me because I am from other country." He also wrote a poem on the front of his book:

Why the humans have to make borders?

Why each country have their own flag?

Why each nation has a different name if we live in the same world?

Why we have to compare with each other when together we can do a lot?

Why we have to live divide for a border if the dirts and air be free?

I think we can live like those things.

Students again divided into groups to prepare presentations on their immigration experiences, including large posters as visuals. Each small group would make their presentation to students from a different class that would be coming in and making the rounds of various small groups in our class. During these presentations, and others, students from the other classes were also prompted to develop questions they would ask, and that teacher shared that list in advance with the student groups so they could also practice their responses. (This is a variation of the community organizing concept of arranging so-called fixed fights—setting people up in a way that success is more likely so they can develop confidence.)

Student stories are also excellent opportunities to help students develop understanding of academic English as well as the ability to use it. The use of Venn diagrams and the terms *compare* and *contrast* are just one example. Another example is helping students use *figurative language* as part of their immigration stories. In addition to their picture books, students wrote and illustrated a *metaphor or simile* to describe their immigration experience. Of course, they first practiced writing similes, including ones like "Love is like a _____ because _____" and "This class is like a _____ because _____."

These beautifully illustrated posters provided some great insights to the conflicting emotions many students had about coming to the United States. Yia wrote, "Coming to the United States was like a bird because a bird can fly anywhere he want." Pa De shared one in the same vein: "Coming to the United States was like a key because opens new doors to success." But there were several like Lisbeth, who wrote, "When I came to the United States was like if I came to a golden cage," and like Mee, who shared, "Coming to the United States was like new shirt because it looks like very beautiful, but when I wear it was not good to wear." Finally, students reviewed and summarized the problems that faced each historical immigrant group they studied—discrimination, economic insecurity, inadequate housing, poor health care, lack of safety,—and were asked if they felt immigrant groups today faced similar problems. Their conclusion was a resounding "Yes!" The rest of the semester the class was focused on what students could do about those problems, including preparing for the U.S. Citizenship Test and becoming active citizens by organizing action to respond to some of the problems they felt they faced today. Those actions will be described later in this chapter.

Students compared their own stories to the stories of the historical immigrant groups, and developed a new interpretation—that in many ways present-day immigrants face many of the same challenges. They had already processed some ideas of how they might respond to those problems. They were ready to take collective action.

And, at the same time, students developed their English skills by learning reading strategies and academic English, content knowledge, oral presentation skills, and new vocabulary—*all in the context of sharing their own stories.* Of course, this interpretation did not occur without planning. Even though an educator/organizer's classroom will run more on the energy of the students than the educator's, we are still not potted plants. We need to set up these learning experiences so that our students can discover knowledge on their own, as this classic story illustrates:

> A father took a son out to the woods one day. As they were walking down a trail, the father saw a deer but didn't say anything. Instead, he continued to walk, and made sure that his son walked on the side of the trail where he could see the deer. "Dad!" the son soon said, "Look, there's a deer over there!" The son was then very alert the rest of the day and saw a number of things that his father didn't notice.

The student projects in this section correlate with California English language development (ELD) domains 1–6.

Venn Diagrams

Student stories can be used in many ways. In a U.S. history class, students drew a five-way Venn diagram exploring the journeys of Columbus, the pilgrims, Lewis and Clark, the Cherokee during the Trail of Tears, and their own travel to the United States. After sharing their diagrams with other students, each one then decided which of the other historical journeys best reflected their own experiences. Vong's poster said, "I am like the traveling of Lewis and Clark because I would like to explore new places and learn new things." Ma's said, "I'm like the Pilgrim's Thanksgiving because I want the freedom of religion like the Pilgrim's like."

The class went on a field trip to a museum garden that was organized to reflect ethnically diverse foods and to the Jelly Belly candy factory. Students shared stories about their families' own garden and dietary experiences, developed Venn diagrams, and converted those diagrams into essays. Through the sequence of sharing stories and developing a new interpretation, some students decided their ethnic food was better for them than American packaged food, and vowed to eat better. Toua titled his essay "The Garden Food Is Natural. The Jelly Belly Food Is Not Healthy."

Students used a Venn diagram in the immigration unit that was discussed earlier in this chapter. Figure 2.1 was done as part of their study of Chinese immigration, and was followed by their converting it into a compare and contrast essay

The student projects in this section correlate with California ELD domains 5 and 6.

K-W-L Charts

K-W-L (what I know, what I want to know, and what I have learned) charts are often used in classrooms prior to beginning a new unit of study. However, in many instances the chart is used like Sergeant Joe Friday's line in the old *Dragnet* television series—"Just the facts." What do you know about the U.S. Civil War? What do you know about New Orleans? These kinds of questions are often not helpful to recent immigrants (and to many native English speakers as well) because they might have little or no prior knowledge about these topics.

However, it was a different story when a teacher asked students to share their knowledge about what happens in a civil war. Vietnamese and Hmong students had many stories to share about Southeast Asia; Guatemalans and Salvadorans told about their family's recent experiences;

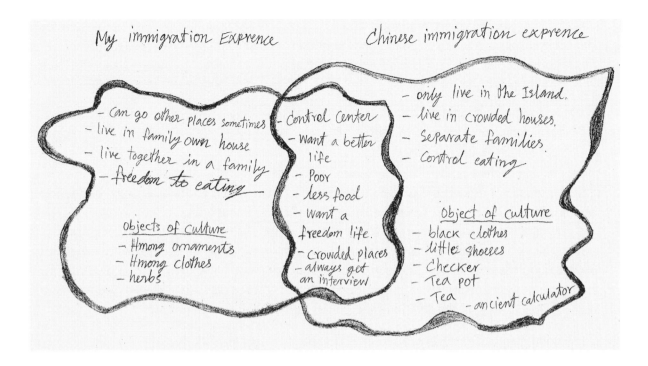

Figure 2.1   Student Venn diagram example.

and many Mexican immigrant students had old family stories about the Mexican Revolution. After sharing these stories, not only was the "K" column filled with real-life examples of what happens in a civil war, but the "W" list was filled with many insightful questions like, "When family members were on different sides, what did they do after the war?" and "Did they ever forget why they were fighting?" They were then very eager to learn about our Civil War. And English language learner students have much to offer native English speakers when they share these experiences. It's one thing to learn about the American Civil War from books. It's an entirely different thing to learn about what happens in a civil war from someone whose family has lived through one.

The same held true, for example, prior to a lesson on New Orleans in geography class. Some students were vaguely familiar with Hurricane Katrina, but many more English language learners could share stories about how devastating hurricanes, monsoons, droughts, tsunamis, or other natural disasters had affected their families. Few had heard of Mardi Gras, but most could think of the wildest holiday celebrations they had in their cultures and native countries. After sharing these stories, again the depth of questions students had about New Orleans and the eagerness they had to learn the answers was pretty remarkable. In both cases, student curiosity was greatly aroused, which is a key ingredient for learning readiness.

The student projects in this section correlate with California ELD domains 1 and 6.

Two-Part Posters

As mentioned earlier, there really are countless opportunities to help students use their stories and develop their intrinsic motivation to learn about a topic and to gain a deeper understanding of content knowledge and the English language. Students made two-part posters of famous women (and other figures) in history. The first part was about a famous woman of their choice. The second part was a story about a person in their own lives who they were reminded of by the famous woman they chose. Mai Tong wrote about the medical pioneer Elisabeth Blackwell. She reminded her of an aunt:

> She is very good about medicine. I remember that she very nice to me. When me or my family and other people was sick she know how to give medicine to us. That time we use Hmong medicine of the nature. She was pass away about many years ago.

Students shared their posters, and then engaged in a lively discussion about what were some common qualities among the women they chose to write about and which ones they felt were most important. Then, out of that list, students reflected about which qualities they felt they had now and which were ones they wanted to develop. The project ended with each student deciding on one thing they could do to help them gain or strengthen a quality within themselves. Once again, that lesson used the sequence of students identifying their own individual stories, then sharing them, followed by coming up with a new interpretation that then led to action. And, of course, during the course of the discussion several new adjectives were learned.

The student projects in this section correlate with California ELD domains 1, 2, 3, 5, and 6.

Family Trees

Early one school year a beginners English class was studying jobs and careers after they had completed a unit on family. The educator asked students to take a simple family tree they had made previously (see the chapter 1) and expand it to include describing both what each family member did for their work and also envision what they would like their own future branch of the tree to look like. Students were able to reinforce and develop their understanding of family and jobs vocabulary. Equally, if not more important, students were able to share with each other stories about which family members did what jobs and why work changed over generations. They were able to discuss their own hopes and concerns, and their plans to overcome those challenges. The Latino, Southeast Asian, and Russian students in the class discovered that they, in fact, had many more similarities than differences. A similar project could be easily differentiated in a mixed-level class, with more advanced students developing these stories, or one of them, into a biographical essay.

The student projects in this section correlate with California ELD domains 1 and 6.

Critical Pedagogy

The critical pedagogy lesson plan is adapted from a Peace Corps teaching guide (Bowman, Larson, Short, McKay, and Valdez-Pierce 64).

Critical Pedagogy Lesson Plan

Instructional Objectives

Students will:

1. Learn academic vocabulary, including the words *fact, problem, solution, similar, describe,* and other words of the teacher's choice (see <http://www.u-46.org/roadmap/dyncat.cfm?cat id=246> for an academic vocabulary word list).

2. Develop cooperative small group skills.

3. Develop critical thinking skills.

4. Practice English-speaking and listening skills.

5. Learn to write grammatically correct sentences.

Duration

Four 55-minute class periods, plus 15 minutes for the following five days.

English Language Development Standards California English Language Development (ELD) Domains

1. Students use English for everyday communication in socially and culturally appropriate ways and apply listening and speaking skills and strategies in the classroom.

5. Students will write well-organized, clear, and coherent text in a variety of academic genres.

6. Students will apply the conventions of standard English usage orally and in writing.

Materials

1. DVD player and DVD of *Les Misérables,* cued to the beginning scene where Jean Valjean steals bread to feed his family or a large image of a man begging for food (or a similar video or image).

2. Copies of this sentence-starter sheet (or posted on the board):

   a. Can you describe what you see? I see _____.

   b. What do you think is the problem? My opinion is (the same/similar/different). I believe _____.

   c. What do you think caused the problem? I believe _____

   d. Have you or your family ever experienced a similar problem? If you have, how did you or your family respond to the problem?

   e. What do you think are other solutions to the problem? My opinion is (the same/similar/different). I believe _____.

3. Poster sheets at least 11" $\times$ 14" for each student

4. Colored markers

5. Old magazines, scissors, and glue (optional)

6. Teacher-prepared model poster

7. Index cards

8. Simple public presentation rubric, including:

Did I do my best on the poster?

Did I look at the audience while I spoke?

Did I speak loudly and clearly?

Procedure

First Day

1. The teacher begins by yawning repeatedly and faking that he is having a hard time keeping his eyes open. Then he asks students to describe to him what they saw (he's wearing a blue shirt, dark pants; he's yawning, stumbling, etc.). He explains that these are facts. He then explains that the class is going to watch a short video clip, and that students will get into small groups of three to describe what they see. He suggests that students might want to take notes.

2. *Les Misérables* clip is shown.

3. Teacher explains that each person will ask the next student in the group the first question in the sentence-starter sheet, and then that person will answer, and so on. Teacher models it with two other students in front of the class and reminds them how they described him earlier. Students are given several minutes to write what they saw. Teacher reminds students to describe only facts.

4. Small groups begin. Teacher circulates and identifies two or three students to share a sentence or two of what they wrote to the entire class when the small group discussion ends.

5. Students share, with teacher writing on overhead transparency or whiteboard what students say. Spend no more than 10 minutes on this part. Students also copy down what is written in front.

6. The teacher then asks students to remember how he was at the beginning of class, and asks what might have caused him to act that way. Students should respond that he was tired, and the teacher clarifies that being tired is a problem. The teacher then asks students to think for a minute if they have ever had the same problem—feeling tired. Next, the teacher asks students to remember their experiences and think for a minute about the questions "How did you respond to the problem? What did you do?" The teacher explains that the next day they are going to get into small groups again and talk about what they think is the problem in the video, what they think caused it, if they have ever had the same problem, and what they did in response to the problem.

Second Day

1. Teacher asks students to think for a minute and remember what they did yesterday. He asks them to share with a neighbor, and then asks one or two students to share with the class.

2. Short video clip is shown again.

3. Teacher demonstrates the meaning of the concepts (and vocabulary) same, similar, and different with a red marker, a red pencil, and a book. He explains that the same small groups are going to answer questions b, c, and d on the sentence starter sheet in the same way they did yesterday. Teacher models with two other students (who have been prepared the day before by the teacher) using the previous day's responses to his problem of being tired and its possible causes. Students are given a few minutes to write down their thoughts.

4. Small groups discuss the problem demonstrated in the movie, its causes, and if they have ever experienced it. Teacher circulates and identifies some students to share with the entire class, and gives them advance notice.

5. Class comes together and shares their conclusions. Teacher writes on a transparency and class copies.

6. Teacher then writes $2 + 2 = $ _____ on the board, and asks students what the answer is. He explains that the answer is also known as the "solution." He asks students if the problem is being tired, what might be different solutions? The "think, pair, share" process is used for responses.

7. Teacher explains that the small groups are going to complete the last answer in the sheet for the problem in the movie, and then make a group poster. The teacher can share a model poster based on his being tired. The top could be labeled "Problem" and simply explain what the problem is: "Being Tired." The bottom could be labeled "Solution" and list the various solutions the class came up with—written in complete sentences. A picture or pictures should illustrate it.

8. Depending on the time available, the small groups can begin answering the final question on this day or the next one. The groups will not report back until their poster is complete.

Third Day

1. Small groups finish the last question and work on their posters.

2. Near the end of class, the teacher explains that the groups will have to present their posters to the class. He distributes index cards, and reviews public speaking skills, including: just write down notes, speak clearly and loudly, make eye contact, and so forth. Teacher models a good presentation and a bad presentation of his poster.

Fourth Day

1. Students are given the beginning of class to complete their posters and practice their presentations, which should only last three or four minutes each with everyone speaking.

2. Presentations begin. Instead of having them all done right after the other, spread them out at the beginning and end of class for two or three days. During each presentation, students who are listening write down what they liked about the presentation. After each presentation, listeners are given a minute to share with a neighbor, and one or two students share with the entire class. Each student presenting completes a rubric and hands it in to the teacher.

Assessment

Students and teacher use the simple public speaking rubric listed earlier. If desired, teacher can develop a similar rubric for students to assess their listening skills. In addition, teachers can create a more detailed rubric appropriate for their classroom situation. Two free online resources to both find premade rubrics and to create ones are University of Wisconsin–Stout: Rubrics for Assessment (<http://www.uwstout.edu/soe/profdev/rubrics.shtml>) and Kathy Shrock's Guide for Educators: Assessment Rubrics (<http://school.discoveryeducation.com/schrockguide/assess.html>).

Possible Extensions/Modifications

1. Student groups could present their posters to another class.

2. If showing a video clip, teacher could have students use the back-to-the-screen exercise, in which half of the class is facing the monitor and half have their backs to it. The clip is shown with no sound and the student watching the video has to describe in English to their partner what is going on in the film. Midway into the clip the roles are reversed. Afterwards, the students can cooperate on writing a description of what they saw.

3. Class could organize some kind of action to respond to hunger issues in their community.

Students are connecting their stories to the story illustrated by the video clip and to the stories of their classmates. They then use those connections to analyze the problem and develop a solution. This lesson can result in the development of critical thinking abilities and academic vocabulary, in addition to improved English writing, speaking, and listening skills. It can be adapted to any problem appropriate for your curriculum at the time—school bullying, refugees, historical crises, and so forth. A video or a still image can be used. The lesson basically follows a six-part process:

1. What do you see?

2. What problem do you think is represented in the picture or video?

3. What do you think caused the problem?

4. Have you or your families ever experienced a similar problem?

5. How did you or your family respond to the problem?

6. What do think are other possible ways to respond to the problem?

Taking Action

After completing the immigration unit mentioned earlier, the class was studying for the U.S. Citizenship Test that many of them would have to take the following year. In addition to learning about the specific questions that might be asked, they were learning what it might take to be an *active* citizen and not just a citizen in legal terms. One of the criteria for active citizenship, the class determined, was to be engaged in improving the community, and one way to begin was to learn about people's concerns.

Each student initiated conversations with 10 other people:

✦ three students within the class,

✦ three students in other classes,

✦ three family members, and

✦ one other adult not part of their family.

They needed to learn several things from these individual meetings. The questions included:

✦ What is this person interested in? How do they spend their time? What gives them energy?

✦ What goals does this person have for next year? Five years from now? Ten years from now?

✦ What does this person worry about?

✦ What other concerns about the community might this person have?

A student teacher and the regular teacher modeled a conversation. The class had periodic check-ins for three weeks. "I like when I came to my family and ask the questions," said Dalila. Lee said, "I liked it because it gave me a chance to go talk with my cousin Diane that I never talk to her for a long time." Some students were having difficulties getting people to be specific with their concerns, so the class discussed how to narrow things down.

There were 29 students in one class, and 20 in another. After 490 of these individual meetings, they shared the results. There were five primary common concerns—getting a good job, affordable housing, passing the citizenship test, crime, and getting a driver's license, with jobs being the biggest one.

As a next step, the classes discussed the difference between a problem and an issue. A problem was big, and difficult to resolve. What would the mayor say to the question, "Can you give us good jobs?" An issue, on the other hand, was specific and achievable in a short period of time. For example, as a first step you could ask the mayor, "Will you assign a staff person to work with us to develop a summer job program for our neighborhood?"

Students formed small groups and worked together to develop examples of how to frame *issues* out of these *problems*. They reviewed notes from their conversations to help pinpoint specific concerns. For housing, one group proposed providing more Section 8 (government-subsidized) rental assistance certificates. For crime, another group proposed more nighttime patrols on one particular street. Reduction of application costs was one idea for citizenship. Several groups suggested wanting to learn more about what job-training opportunities might be available.

The class concluded they wanted to take some kind of action, and decided to focus on job-training opportunities. One of the students' brothers attended a job training program, and obtained some information about it. They learned that the school district itself had a major job training center not too far from their school, and it had several classes where students were paid while they were being trained. Through a conversation with a staff person there, students also learned that the center was part of a consortium of job training providers that had another center just two blocks from the school. This staff person agreed to bring representatives from a variety of programs to a meeting at the school that students would organize. Students also learned that taxes paid by their families and themselves supported these agencies—this was not charity.

During this entire period, students role-played speaking, wrote and completed clozes (fill-in-the-blank exercises), and used specific reading strategies. Students learned adjectives, and developed political strategy, by brainstorming about how they wanted the invited officials to describe the students to their colleagues and friends after the meeting ("I went to a meeting at Burbank High School today, and they were _____." Students came up with the words "good listeners, very interested, organized, powerful.")

Students planned the meeting, contacted all the people they had spoken with, and practiced what they would say. One-hundred-and-fifty people attended the multilingual gathering, led by the students. In the evaluation afterwards, Ma said she learned "that they have many programs to help the people who have no education," and many others echoed her. Students were unanimous also in their feeling that the best part of the meeting, though, was, as Mee put it, "because we have many students to speak."

Having students connect their personal stories to academic content can help them create personal meaning. This can increase the likelihood of new knowledge being placed in long-term memory, as well as enhancing intrinsic motivation. These are good results in themselves. However, it's the sharing of these stories, the give-and-take of developing interpretations, and, finally, the movement toward taking action, where the deeper learning takes place. The former without the latter is like knowing the words. The two together is like knowing the words *and* hearing the music.

Explicit language development activities are integral to all of the lessons mentioned:

+ Echo reading (students repeating parts of sentences that the educator reads from short read-alouds about the lesson);

+ paired reading (students are divided into pairs and take turns reading to each other sections of expository text about the topic);

+ highlighting words in the reading that illustrate a particular phonic or grammar example;

+ using sentence scrambles (picking sentences from the text or student stories and mixing up the order);

+ playing games like "Telephone" (Where the class is divided in half and the first person in each group is told a sentence about the topic. Then the same sentence has to be whispered correctly one-by-one to the last person);

+ practicing to write a five-paragraph essay; and

+ completing sequencing activities with unit-related texts. The passage is cut-up and students need to place the pieces in the correct order.

These are just a few language development exercises that are made particularly effective by being used during the storytelling sequence.

The student projects in this section correlate with California ELD domains 1, 2, 3, and 6.

How Can Technology Be Used to Access Prior Knowledge through Stories?

Students can also use technology to help tell their stories. As mentioned earlier, there are many free sites that students can use on the Internet (listed in Appendix 1) to create these digital storytelling presentations with maps, images, photos, and text. These can certainly be utilized in place of the color pen and construction paper presentations, or just plain paper and pen, that students often use. However, using technology does not automatically add much value to this story-telling process. It does create an opportunity for students to develop computer skills, it can be a neat vehicle for students to share their creations at home (if their families have computer access), and it also can function as a good change of pace. If used appropriately, the computer can be a major asset in developing writing skills—in large part because of its automatic spelling and grammar functions. Finally, in the context of being connected to sister classes in other parts of the world, online student projects can be shown on a Web site or a blog and shared with an authentic audience in other parts of the country or throughout the world. Students in both classes can then respond with online written and/or audio comments. Resources on where to make these kinds of connections can be found in Appendix 1.

In addition to creating audio-narrated slideshows and the other benefits already mentioned, there are other exceptional ways students can use technology to tell their stories that clearly do add a great deal of value to the process—especially for English language learners. One is through the use of one of two Web sites—YAKiToME (<http://yakitome.com/>) or Read the Words (<http://readthewords.com/>). Using these sites, students can upload in seconds an essay or story they have written. Then, seconds later, either one of these sites is hosting the essay online so that it's accessible from any computer in the world with an Internet connection. (Of course, with this tool—and with any other one mentioned in this book—students should use only their first names and not provide sensitive personal information.) But the key element is that it provides audio as well. Any English language learner student, a family member, or a friend can go to the site and read along with the text as a reasonably human-sounding computer-generated voice reads the words. The first chapter in this book described the importance of providing high-interest accessible reading material to English language learners. It doesn't get much higher interest to students and their families than their own stories.

There are also several Web tools, including Vocaroo (<http://vocaroo.com/>), Screentoaster (<http://www.screentoaster.com/record>), and Daft Doggy (<http://www.daftdoggy.com/recorder/record.php>) that let students easily record their own voices to narrate their online projects.

It's also probable that by the time you read this book, many other similar sites with even more advanced capabilities will be online. School librarians might be uniquely suited to explore new applications and their use in education.

The student projects in this section correlate with California ELD domains 1, 5, and 6.

How Do You Assess Accessing Prior Knowledge through Stories?

As in the case of building relationships, a substantial body of research, particularly related to brain-based learning, demonstrates that using student stories brings many educational benefits. These include helping students create personal meaning of new information and thereby allowing knowledge to be more easily moved to long-term memory. Another benefit is that student stories provide an effective arena in which students can develop specific language skills. It also, at least theoretically, should help reduce classroom stress through deepening student relationships.

What do students say about using this storytelling and storymaking process in our classroom? After reviewing the lessons done during the year or semester that involved storytelling and storymaking, one way to assess its success is to ask them to respond anonymously to the following questions: "Did you like sharing your stories? Why or why not? What, if anything, did you learn from sharing your stories?"

Here are a few typical responses:

✦ Yes, because it teaches me about other people life. I learned how to be a better person.

✦ Yes, because it helps me talk better. It helps me learned how to read better.

✦ I likes to do these projects because it helps many things, like words, reading and talking.

✦ Yes, I learned how to love my life by doing these projects.

✦ Yes, I learned about how other people live their life. I learned about love.

✦ It helps me learn many new words and to talk better.

✦ Yes, because I know how to write a sentence.

✦ I liked because I was able to express what myself think and feel.

✦ I like to share my story to other students and like to hear about their stories, too. We had similar experiences.

✦ I like to share story because I learn many things from others. I learned how do they live. I learned what they like. I learned what they plan for their life.

The research, combined with these kinds of student evaluations, gives a good indication that the storytelling and storymaking part of the organizing cycle is an effective teaching and learning strategy.

What Are the Challenges to Accessing Prior Knowledge through Stories in the Classroom?

As with all the elements of the organizing cycle, there are challenges to getting started and to being successful in implementing the idea of sharing and interpreting stories.

Listening and Engaging

One challenge is to help our students understand that storytelling is not just students sharing their experiences and having others listen. If we are to help our students work together to develop new and deeper interpretations of what happens in their lives, we have to also help them develop listening and engaging skills. The reading strategies in chapter 4 in this book help students to bring meaning to what they read. They have to do the same as they listen to personal stories. They need to be able to make personal connections, visualize, summarize, synthesize, and ask questions as they listen to the stories of their classmates. As in the individual meetings that were focused on building relationships, the use of storytelling needs to be more of an exchange and less an imparting of information. Modeling, a critical part of most effective teaching, is particularly important here.

Taking Care of Ourselves

In order to be successful educator/organizers, we also have to be consistent about taking time for ourselves and getting refreshed.

In his book, *7 Habits of Highly Effective People,* Stephen Covey writes that "Sharpen the Saw" is the seventh habit and the one that makes all the other ones possible. He tells this story:

Suppose you were to come upon someone in the woods working feverishly to saw down a tree. "What are you doing?" you ask. "Can't you see?" comes the impatient reply. "I'm sawing down this tree." "You look exhausted!" you exclaim, "How long have you been at it?" "Over five hours," he returns, "and I'm beat! This is hard word" "Well, why don't you take a break for a few minutes and sharpen that saw?" you inquire, "I'm sure it would go a lot faster." "I don't have time to sharpen the saw," the man says emphatically, "I'm too busy sawing!" (Covey 287)

English language learner teachers can sharpen their saws by both being intentional about maintaining a healthy work/personal balance and by developing a network of professional support.

Tech Tip: Personal Learning Networks

The idea of personal learning networks (PLNS), a group of colleagues with whom you can gain and give support and professional advice, is certainly not a new idea. These kinds of connections have long been used by people in all kinds of professions, including among educators. Now, however, the Web offers incredible opportunities to expand these PLNs. Teachers of English language learners all over the world have created simple online networks to connect using Web applications like Twitter, e-mail listservs, blogs, and social networks. "The Best Ways ESL/EFL/ELL Teachers Can Develop Personal Learning Networks" (<http://larryferlazzo.edublogs. org/2009/11/07/the-best-ways-esleflell-teachers-can-develop-personal-learning-networks/>) contains a list of these resources.

A well-known quote is commonly attributed to Dr. Dale E. Turner: "When Goliath came against the Israelites, the soldiers all thought, 'He's so big, we can never kill him.' But David looked at the same giant and thought, 'He's so big I can't miss him.'"

Our students are filled to the brim with vast quantities of stories. It can be scary and risky to elicit stories from our students, to help them learn to become good listeners, and to guide them as they develop the capacity to become interpreters and storymakers. But our students are filled with *so* many personal experiences and stories that have *so* much potential that, with a little effort, we can't miss turning these stories into tremendous learning opportunities.

CHAPTER 3

Identifying and Mentoring Students' Leadership Potential

During the class time when students were reading books of their choice, I went around and had short individual conversations with five students. We were studying U.S. history and women's suffrage, and I explained that the next day we were going to read about and watch a short video clip showing demonstrators being attacked nearly 100 years ago for supporting a woman's right to vote. I told each of the five that I thought they were leaders—that other students looked up to them—and that I would like them to help lead a small group discussion following the video. Students would be discussing questions like, "Why do you think men attacked the women demonstrators?" and "Have you or your parents ever been attacked, verbally or physically, for doing something you believed in?" I asked them to read ahead of time the short piece in our textbook that we would be discussing, and think of any additional questions that would be good to ask the small group to answer.

The leaders' job would be to make sure that everyone in the group understood the questions, got a chance to talk, and spoke English. In addition, they would need to help prepare someone else—not them—from their group to make a brief report to the entire class. That would mean they would want to have the reporter practice in the group, and elicit encouraging comments from other group members. I referred back to a lesson we had recently done with another class creating a Venn diagram comparing the leadership skills of South Africa's Nelson Mandela and the Hmong's General Vang Pao—students had concluded that one of the things they both did was help train new leaders.

I told each of them that if they didn't want to be group leaders I would accept their decision, but that I knew they could do it and I would be available to help. Each of the five agreed to do it.

The next day one of the students came to me and suggested adding the question, "Have you ever felt like attacking someone else for what they believed or did?" It was a good one, and I added it to the list.

We went through the lesson and, though the small groups were a little uneven, it all went pretty well.

After class, Jose, who had not been one of the small group leaders, came up to me and asked, "Mr. Ferlazzo, do you think I could be a leader sometime when we have groups?" I assured him he could, and told him I was pleased that he saw himself as a leader, as I did.

The following day I checked in with the five small group leaders to see how they felt about their work. They all said they liked doing it, and particularly liked preparing the reporter. After I asked them if there was anything they felt they could have done better, a couple of students who led the groups that were a little uneven said they felt they could have pushed the more quiet people to talk a little more.

I individually made a proposition (invitation) to students, and explained why I was doing so and what the job entailed. I referred back to what they had concluded earlier about the importance of leaders developing new leaders. I also invited students to help make the lesson their own by adding their own questions. Each student was given the option of saying no—as mentioned previously, if you don't give people the opportunity to say no, then they really don't have the opportunity to say yes, either. There were now five other people in the room besides me who felt their job was to help people learn, work together, and develop new leaders. Their modeling encouraged another student to say he would like a chance to do the same next time. And the five learned they liked helping others develop new skills and learned what they could do better as leaders.

What Do You Mean by Identifying and Mentoring Students' Leadership Potential?

The goal of community organizing is to help people develop civic skills and the ability to acquire power, which most dictionaries define as "the ability to act." There are different kinds of power, including individual and collective power. In terms of achieving long-term, healthy, and transformative change, organizers believe that people must feel like they have their own sense of power *and* that organizing collectively can ultimately result in the most individual *and* collective benefit.

What does power have to do with student leadership development?

Warren Bennis, the scholar, author, and a pioneer in leadership studies, writes, "Leadership is the wise use of power. Power is the capacity to translate intention into reality and sustain it" (Bennis and Naus 31). In other words, you really can't be a leader without having power.

Coincidentally, or perhaps not so coincidentally, many of the same qualities community organizers view as essential to be a good leader have been identified by researchers as equally important qualities to be a good language learner. These qualities include being intrinsically motivated, being willing to take risks and learn from your mistakes, being willing to engage with and teach others (since we learn best what we teach), and, importantly, having a strong sense of self-efficacy (a strong belief in oneself that one can accomplish one's goals). William Glasser calls this last quality *"power within"* (Erwin 100). By cultivating these qualities in students, educators accomplish two goals.

The first is that students develop skills that can enhance their ability to learn English. The second is that, since several of these qualities are considered the so-called soft skills needed to participate in public life (the same skills, according to many business leaders, that are also needed by workers entering the job force), by cultivating these skills we help to more effectively prepare our students to be active citizens in a democracy *and* to be more successful in their future employment.

Though a goal of all the classroom examples shared in this book is to help students develop a greater sense of self-efficacy, this chapter will include ones that are specifically designed to accomplish that goal. In addition, this chapter will also share strategies to help students develop another kind of power through developing leadership abilities—what Glasser calls *"power with"* (Erwin 100) and organizers call "relational power." This is the power of collective action, and the ability to engage with others in order to initiate and cultivate it.

We want our students to do their individual work well. At the same time, we can help them—especially those who feel particularly isolated by being in a new country with a new language—develop the leadership and people skills they need to become active citizens in a democracy and reach their full potential. This can, in turn, result in their doing the individual work even better.

The word "leader" comes from the Old English word "lithan," which means "to go." By including leadership development as one of our teaching goals, we can assist our students to go much further—academically, socially, and economically—than they could have without this kind of preparation.

If we do not keep these soft skills in mind, and just accept the notion that information alone is power, we increase the likelihood that our students will someday be like the man who misreads his situation in this paraphrased folktale:

> A man went to the mountain and told it, "You're not very smart. You don't know how big you are, how you are shaped, what you are made of. But I, just a man, know everything about you!" The mountain replied, "You're right, but I *am* the mountain."

What Does Research Say about Leadership Development in the Classroom?

Quite a bit of research has been done on what makes a good language learner. Many of these conclusions might hold true for what makes a good learner . . . period. As already mentioned, these qualities are often a match with what a community organizer looks for in a leader, too.

Intrinsically Motivated

Community organizers are often asked, "How do you get people motivated?" Many would answer, "We don't motivate people. We help people figure out what they can use to motivate themselves."

This is eerily similar to what Edward Deci, one of the premier researchers and authorities on intrinsic motivation, wrote, "The proper question is not, 'how can people motivate others?' but rather, *'how can people create the conditions within which others will motivate themselves*?'" (Deci 10).

Being intrinsically motivated means doing something because of being interested in the task—it helps one accomplish a self-directed goal, or it brings pleasure, or it's a stimulating challenge. Researchers have long identified the importance of a second language learner having this kind of motivation—which leads to lasting change over the longer term—as opposed to being primarily motivated by extrinsic rewards or punishments, which tends toward short-term gains:

> first, motivation must emanate from the learner . . . second, learners must see themselves as agents of the processes that shape their motivation. After all, as long as motivation is externally regulated and controlled by the teacher, learners cannot be expected to develop skills in regulating their own motivation on which good language learning depends. (Griffiths 31)

There are many ways teachers can help foster intrinsic motivation in students. By helping to identify student self-interests we can help students identify their own goals as much as possible and help them work toward achieving them. This helps students develop a sense of autonomy—"that their actions are their own choice" (Deci 87). This feeling of having choices in the classroom is critical to developing intrinsic motivation. Most English language learner students had very little power in the choice to move to a new country with a new culture and new language. In light of this likely sense of powerlessness, it's particularly important for teachers of English language learners to provide as many options as possible to their students.

At the same time learners need to develop a sense of autonomy, English language learners' desire to "negotiate entry into the desired social networks" (Griffiths 24) is often another source of intrinsic motivation. Much research has shown that cooperative learning can develop these kinds of connections (Rogers, Ludington, and Graham 12) that can promote intrinsic motivation (Griffiths 28).

Beginning English language learners often can increase their language ability quickly. As they advance, however, motivational challenges increase:

> As language proficiency develops, the learning demands grow exponentially in terms of cognitive and linguistic complexity, and skill and activity range, while any pay-off for the learning effort expended in terms of increased mastery becomes less and less tangible. Sadly, research all too often points to a steady decline in levels of motivation. (Griffiths 26)

This decline emphasizes the importance of teachers using strategies to enhance intrinsic motivation.

A Sense of Self-Efficacy, Willingness to Take Risks, and Willingness to Learn from Mistakes

A sense of self-efficacy (which could also be called self-confidence or self-esteem), a willingness to take risks, and then the ability to learn from mistakes that might occur as a result have been shown time and time again in research to be important qualities in second language learning: "Good language learners are not necessarily those to whom a language comes easily;

but they have persevered, have overcome frustrations, and have, after many trials and errors, achieved a satisfactory level of proficiency" (Stern 380).

Researchers have also emphasized the importance of learners having high self-esteem and its connection to a willingness to take risks. Krashen quotes noted language researcher and author H. D. Brown as concluding that "the person with high self-esteem is able to reach out beyond himself more freely, to be less inhibited, and because of his ego strength, to make the necessary mistakes involved in language learning with less threat to his ego" (Krashen, "Second Language Acquisition" 23).

Teachers can help students develop their self-confidence through several ways. One is through the development of a supportive community of learners as was discussed in the first chapter. Another is through teaching learning strategies.

This idea is different from teaching skills (for example, how to pronounce a word). We want to teach strategies, such as how to pronounce a word even if the student has never seen it before. Skills are how to turn on the ignition in a car. A strategy is what you do if you've lost your car keys. "Self-efficacious learners feel confident about solving a problem because they have developed an approach to problem solving that has worked" (National Capital Language Resource Center 2). A National Capital Language Resource Center study showed that the more language learners used learning strategies, the more they "perceived themselves as more confident in their language-learning abilities" (National Capital Language Resource Center 5).

The next chapter, "Learning by Doing," will go into more detail, but these strategies can include using graphic organizers, using cognates, using background knowledge, and so forth.

Willingness to Teach Others

Finally, good learners in general, including second language learners, also teach others. Dr. William Glasser has often quoted Edgar Dale's "Cone of Experience" (<http://www.greenspun.com/bboard/q-and-a-fetch-msg.tcl?msg_id=00AV58>): "We learn 10% of what we read, 20% of what we hear, 30% of what we see, 50% of what we see and hear, 70% of what we say or write . . . [and] 90% of what we teach" (Dale 107). Teaching others not only forces students to make several more touches (rereading of the material) on learned material, but it enhances self-confidence and provides good modeling for other students. When done well, this strategy can also help students develop the kinds of relationships that organizers believe are critical for genuine leaders to have—those that are needed in order to move people into collective action. In these kinds of relationships, people have respect for the judgment of leaders and feel that they can offer something they need. After all, how can someone truly be considered a leader if they do not have a following?

In an article written for *Education Week,* Debra Viadero describes studies examining peer-teaching techniques. A 2003 analysis of more than 80 studies on peer-assisted learning found that peer tutoring was effective, and the effects were strongest for "students who were younger, in inner-city schools, from poor families, or members of minority groups." Analysis of another 36 studies concluded that "students taking part in peer-teaching activities spent more time on task, exhibited better social skills, and expressed more motivation and less frustration than counterparts in teacher-directed classrooms."

Research in Action

This skill of *teaching others* can be reinforced by such activities as having English language learners teach other classes about what they have learned about a particular topic (or about other areas of their cultural or experiential knowledge); through jigsaw activities (where small groups of students take different parts of an article or topic and teach the rest of the class about it); through periodically strategically grouping students with a higher English proficiency level with those with a lower level; through the use of a system (or variation of it) that Charles Greenwood, Carmen Arreaga-Mayer, Cheryl A. Utley, Karen M. Gavin, and Barbara J. Terry called a "ClassWide Peer Tutoring Learning Management System," which pairs up students regardless of proficiency level and has been shown to be effective with English language learners; and even through student displays in school libraries specifically designed to teach a topic.

According to Ricardo Schütz, Krashen's perspective on second language learning asserts that language learners have an "affective filter," a sort of barrier that when raised makes language acquisition difficult and when lowered makes it easier. Being willing to engage with others, to take risks and learn from mistakes, and having a sense of self-confidence all contribute to lowering this barrier.

What Are Classroom Examples of Leadership Development?

Obviously, not all of our students will come to us, or leave us, with strengths in all of these leadership qualities. Students come to us wanting to learn English. We can share with them what the research says about what good language learners do. We can't *make* them have intrinsic motivation, take risks, have self-confidence, or want to teach others. We can, however, agitate them to work on developing these attributes. We can help students think about their learning—their metacognition—and see if they can connect with their own inner motivation to become as effective English language learners, and leaders, that they can be. And we, as educators, must be strategic about how we help guide them in this journey.

Making the Qualities of a Good Learner and Leader Explicit

One first goal might be to make sure that early in the school year all students demonstrate that they have at least a little bit of each one of these qualities—without labeling each quality at the time. In one early lesson students can be asked to describe orally and in writing some of what they consider to be the most important and the most enjoyable (obviously, not necessarily the same) learning experiences in their lives—and what drove them to learn them. A lesson on learning about the scientific method can include sharing an experience where they learned from a mistake they made. One of the activities mentioned in chapter 1 was having students make a poster describing things they are good at. And as for teaching others, students can do projects with other classes where they have to prepare a lesson plan and teach it, and many small group activities like the one that opened this chapter could take place where individual students take leadership roles.

After these tasks are accomplished in the first two or three months of the school year, the educator could then share the list of what qualities the research says makes a good language learner and, in fact, a good learner—period. Teachers can lead a class discussion highlighting how everyone in the class has shown that they have each quality, so they are certainly on the road to success. Each student then can be asked to think about one quality he or she wants to work on improving over the next quarter. During various times of individual class work, including if there is a regular period for students to read books of their choice, the teacher can have a short conversation with each student during which he or she will share what he or she has concluded and then make a plan of action. Each quarter thereafter students can evaluate how they've done on improving that quality in themselves. The class can revisit the list of qualities periodically during the year, and students can share other qualities they think make a good language learner.

It is still not time to explicitly talk much about students being leaders and taking leadership roles, however, because many might still be intimidated by the prospect. The next step is studying a very short unit on leadership where the class does language-development activities using:

✦ short read-alouds,

✦ five-minute snippets of videos,

✦ clozes (fill-in-the-blank),

✦ make-and-breaks (sequencing activities, which will be discussed more in the next chapter), and

✦ folktales and news articles that illustrate examples the qualities of a good learner—building relationship, taking risks, making mistakes, feeling confidence, and teaching others.

During these activities, the good language learner qualities can be shown in the context of being a good leader. The historical leaders and stories used might depend on the ethnicity of students to enhance the personal connection as much as possible. A teacher might use a vignette from the life of César Chávez, or the Mexican leader Emilio Zapata, or a Vietnamese folktale. School librarians might be especially helpful in identifying appropriate biographical incidents and stories. Students can also share stories that illustrate one or more of these qualities in people they know personally and who they consider leaders.

The educator can draw out from students the qualities these leaders had, and then students themselves are usually able to see the similarities between the qualities of a good language learner and the qualities of a leader. Of course, it helps when the lists are right next to each other at the front of the classroom!

Then the educator can begun a discussion about students as leaders. This kind of discussion waits until after several phases are completed:

First, all students have had an opportunity to successfully demonstrate they have these qualities.

Second, the class discusses these qualities in the context of being a good language learner.

Third, students discover for themselves that these qualities are also present in leaders whom we study and others whom they know.

Fourth, students discuss the questions "Are you a leader?" and "Do you want to be a leader?" in the context of their own lives.

It is possible, if not probable, that talking to students about being leaders prior to going through this process can provoke a strong negative reaction to the idea that they are a leader. By carefully planning strategically (strategic planning is more "ready, aim, fire" as opposed to "ready, fire, aim") educators are able to usually generate much more positive feedback to this idea.

The student projects in this section correlate with California English language development (ELD) domains 1, 2, 3, 4, and 6.

Choices and Power

You can't really be a leader without having power. William Glasser considers power to be a basic need of students, and writes that 95 percent of classroom management issues occur as a result of students trying to fulfill this need for power (Ryan and Cooper 85). This sense of power (remember its definition—"the ability to act") is particularly important to English language learner students, many of whom have been uprooted from their native countries through no choice of their own, face challenges in basic understanding and communicating in our culture's primary language, and are often living in lower-income communities where examples of powerlessness are obvious each day.

Democracy in the Classroom

One way to do this in the classroom is to invite students to participate in making decisions and choices since the availability of choices cultivates the development of intrinsic motivation. One can create a more democracy-centered class by considering the following:

Room design

> Educators could become less invested in having the classroom or school library look the way they want, and more interested in having it reflect more of the students' desires.

Grading

> Have students grade their own work using a simple rubric.

Classroom Story

I have had students grade their own work for the past six years. Ninety percent of the time I leave the grade as is. Five percent of the time I raise it. Five percent of the time the student and I jointly decide to lower it after a discussion.

Field trips

> An educator can offer list of different options for field trips during the year, and students decide which ones we should do. In addition, after jointly developing a field trip criteria, students can voice suggestions for other ideas of field trips that they would like to take.

Tech Tip—Virtual Field Trips

If money is a problem, another option is taking a free, virtual field trip. These are done over the Internet and typically fall into one of four categories:

- Trips are sponsored by an organization or public agency, and they have hosts who will take your class and others on a trip—through a nature sanctuary, an ancient ruin—that can be watched on a screen through your computer projector. Generally these are live, educators have to sign up for them in advance, and they offer the ability for students to ask questions via a microphone or texting on a computer.
- Trips are recorded and set up to give a virtual multimedia tour on the Internet whenever you want to use it.
- Educators set up trips on their own. With Web sites providing countless panoramic images and multimedia resources, teachers can just create a list of the ones they want to use. Using Google Earth software, if available, is one of many options.
- Students, working in small groups, set up their own trips after having experienced one as a model.

See Appendix 1 for more information.

Classroom management

When there is a classroom management issue with a student or with the entire class, an educator can ask the student or the class for ideas on how to resolve it and/or provide several options (always more than two) from which the student or class could choose.

Games

A list of classroom games used to reinforce lessons is in Appendix 2. Involve students in deciding which ones they want to play.

Unit order

If feasible, share with students the different units that will be covered over the next couple of months or longer, and let them decide the order in which they want to study them.

Seats

Give students the option of where they want to sit, or at least hear what their preferences might be prior to making a decision.

These are just a few ideas, and every day an educator has countless opportunities to help students develop their senses of power, intrinsic motivation, and self-confidence. In order to do this, however, an educator needs to recognize that power is not a finite pie. If an educator helps his or her students gain some power, it does not mean the educator has less. In fact, through the sharing of power, many more possibilities for learning are created. It's important for educators to model that concept, and also help students understand that while having self-confidence is an important leadership element, being egotistical and feeling like you can do everything on your own is not an effective model of leadership, learning, or for a way of living one's life.

The student projects in this section correlate with California ELD domain 1.

I Feel Powerful When . . .

In the "I feel powerful when . . ." lesson, students are asked to make a list of times when they felt powerful in their lives using the sentence starter "I feel powerful when . . ."

"I Feel Powerful When . . ." Lesson Plan

Instructional Objectives

Students will:

1. Practice English-speaking and listening skills in small group work.

2. Develop categorization skills.

3. Gain an understanding of cooperative leadership.

4. Learn new vocabulary.

Duration

Two-and-one-half or three 55-minute class periods.

English Language Development Standards California English Language Development (ELD) Domains

1. Students use English for everyday communication in socially and culturally appropriate ways and apply listening and speaking skills and strategies in the classroom.

6. Students will apply the conventions of standard English usage orally and in writing.

Materials

1. Copies for all students of sentences they wrote completing the "I feel powerful when . . ." sentence starters, along with list of teacher-suggested category titles.

2. Blank sheets of 11" $\times$ 14" paper, glue, scissors, and color markers.

3. Copies of a simple rubric to be completed by students on the categorization project:

    a. Did I follow instructions in making my poster?

    b. Is the poster complete?

    c. Do the underlined words truly show evidence of their category choices?

Procedure

First Day

1. Teacher writes the word "power" on the board, and explains that power means "you can get things done," then explains that you feel "powerful" when you have power. She gives some examples, perhaps reading a book and feeling powerful because she can understand the words; feeling powerful when she is successful in helping a student understand something new; and feeling powerful when she plays basketball and has a good game. Feeling this kind of self-confidence is a quality of a good language learner.

2. Teacher asks students to think about times when they felt powerful, when they felt self-confident and felt that they could get things done. She asks students to write down at least three times they felt that way (students at a lower English level could also draw scenes instead). Teacher circulates to help ensure students understand the word "powerful."

3. Students are divided into groups of three to share what they wrote. Teacher identifies students with particularly good examples and tells them she will call on them to share with the entire class.

4. After small groups are finished, teacher asks students to share.

5. Teacher then tells students to pick one of the examples they wrote down, or another new one they have just remembered. Each student is given a poster sheet and markers to write their sentences down in big letters and illustrate them if there is time.

6. Teacher collects sheets.

7. After class, teacher types the sentences the students wrote, numbers them, and makes copies for each student. The teacher also identifies at least four categories (for example, "learning something," "teaching others," "doing something well," "when people listen to me") that the sentences would fit into and tries to word them in a way that's connected to the quality of a good language learner and leader. The teacher makes sure that the sentences are mixed up and are not organized by category. Student posters, if possible, are tacked on the classroom wall.

Second Day

1. The teacher places a pencil, book, marker, notebook, and a pen on a front table where all students can see it.

2. Teacher holds up the pencil, and then asks the class "Is this pencil like this notebook?" Class responds no. "Is this pencil like this book?" Class responds no. "Is this pencil like a marker?" Class responds yes, and teacher puts the pencil and marker together. Teacher follows a similar process for each item and ends up with two "piles"—the book and notebook in one and the pen, pencil and marker in the other. Teacher asks how the book and notebook are similar, and students can respond they both have paper. Teacher writes "Have paper" (or something similar) about them. Teacher does the same with the other pile, probably writing "You can write with them" on a sheet for that pile. Teacher explains that each is a category—a group that various things fit into.

3. Each student is given the sheet containing all their sentences (called a data set) with the list of categories either on the paper or just written on the front board. Teacher explains, using a transparency, that students will be using a similar process to place their sentences into the categories. The teacher leads the class in identifying which category is appropriate for the first three sentences, and explains that students are to:

   ✦ Work with a partner.

   ✦ Cut out each sentence, being sure to include the number.

   ✦ Underline the one or two words in each sentence that support their decision to place the sentence in that category (the teacher demonstrates this in the first three sentences).

   ✦ Glue the sentences under the title of each category on the poster sheet.

4. While students are working, the teacher will identify two students who are completing the assignment successfully. The teacher will tell each student that she is going to call on them to just list out the numbers they have placed in one category. In the middle of the assignment, the teacher asks for everyone's attention and calls on each of the two students to list just the numbers for one category, which the teacher writes on the board. The teacher then

asks everyone to think for a minute and look at their sheet and be ready to say what category they think the sentences belong to. After a minute the teacher calls on one student to respond and then asks the student who gave the numbers if that is the correct category.

5. Teacher reviews the sentences and categories with the entire class, if time.

Third Day

1. Teacher completes class review of categorization, being sure to be open to students placing the sentences into different categories if they can provide a good justification.

2. Teacher explains that we all can feel powerful in different ways and be particularly strong in certain qualities—imagine if a group of people who felt powerful in different ways came together and imagine the things they could accomplish. The teacher could explain: "Juan could be a computer genius and spend thousands of hours inventing a great video game; Pa has some money that she is willing to risk to loan him to manufacture it, and I could write a manual explaining to people how to play it. Together, we are strong in different qualities and can accomplish something that we could not do separately. We become allies."

Assessment

Students will complete the simple rubric and turn it in along with their posters. In addition, teachers can create a more detailed rubric appropriate for their classroom situation. Two free online resources both to find premade rubrics and to create new ones are University of Wisconsin–Stout: Rubrics for Assessment (<http://www.uwstout.edu/soe/profdev/rubrics. shtml>) and Kathy Shrock's Guide for Educators: Assessment Rubrics (<http://school.discovery education.com/schrockguide/assess.html>).

Possible Extensions/Modifications

Student can ask family members for examples of when they felt powerful and then share them in class.

Here is a data set example that was used in this lesson:

"I feel powerful when . . ." data set

Categories

Having Enough Money

Having Knowledge and Being Able to Do Things with It

Helping People

People Listen to Me and Respect Me

Doing Your Best

1. . . . I have a lot of money.

2. . . . I have a great job.

3. . . . I am a leader.

4. . . . I am a teacher

5. . . . I feel people like me.

6. . . . I know how to read and write in English.

7. . . . I say something and other people listen to me.

8. . . . people believe in me.

9. . . . many people agree with me.

10. . . . I can do whatever I want

11. . . . my mom and dad say they love me.

12. . . . I get an A in class.

13. . . . I do a presentation and other students listen.

14. . . . I teach reading to my sisters.

15. . . . I have knowledge.

16. . . . I am captain of my soccer team.

17. . . . I win a competition.

18. . . . I help other people.

19. . . . I take care of my children.

20. . . . I drive a car.

21. . . . I do something good.

22. . . . I get all I want.

23. . . . I play with other people and I'm the best player.

24. . . . I have more money to buy things I want to buy.

25. . . . I read a book.

The most important part of the lesson comes in the last discussion on what is possible by developing allies and working together. We want to encourage our students to not be timid and, instead, take risks. At the same time, however, we want them to learn (and this is a lesson that many of us need to be reminded of as well), not to be reckless. This lesson of building allies reinforces both key concepts and helps students understand that they do not have to necessarily be exceptional in all of the key qualities, as few of us are.

Learning Strategies

By teaching learning strategies, we can help students develop the confidence and ability to monitor their own learning and have a full toolbox of strategies to call upon when needed. A list of 20 such strategies can be found in Figure 3.1.

Reading strategies—asking questions, visualizing, summarizing, making connections, and evaluating—are also learning strategies. Here is one simple and effective way to teach them.

After reading a short passage together, the educator can distribute small whiteboards (which can be purchased inexpensively or even made), markers, and erasers to each student. After reading certain passages, the educator models one strategy. For example, after reading, "Ben drove his car to the store," he might model the asking questions strategy by writing on the

Strategy	Teacher	Learner
Background Knowledge	Activate your students' prior knowledge in order to build new material on what they already know.	Think about what you already know about a topic to help you learn more about it.
Personalize	Through discussion, link new material to your students' experiences and feelings using guiding questions or other activities.	Link new material to your personal experiences and feelings.
Summarize	Have your students read a text, then summarize it to aid comprehension.	After you read a text, stop a moment and summarize the meaning to help your comprehension
Use Imagery	Create a meaningful context for your students by accompanying new information with figures, illustrations, and photographs.	Associate new information with a mental or printed image to help you learn it.

METACOGNITIVE STRATEGIES		
Strategy	**Description**	
Organize / Plan	Calendar	→ Plan the task or content sequence. → Set goals. → Plan how to accomplish the task.
Manage Your Own Learning	Pace Yourself	→ Determine how you learn best. → Arrange conditions that help you learn. → Seek opportunities for practice. → Focus your attention on the task.
Monitor	Check	While working on a task: → Check your progress on the task. → Check your comprehension as you use the language. Are you understanding? → Check your production as you use the language. Are you making sense?

Figure 3.1 Learning strategies chart. (continued)
Reprinted with permission from the National Foreign Language Resource Center.

Evaluate	I did it!	After completing a task: → Assess how well you have accomplished the learning task. → Assess how well you have applied the strategies. → Decide how effective the strategies were in helping you accomplish the task.

TASK BASED STRATEGIES: USE WHAT YOU KNOW		
Strategy	**Description**	
Use Background Knowledge	I know.	→ Think about and use what you already know to help you do the task. → Make associations.
Make Inferences	Use Clues	→ Use context and what you know to figure out meaning. → Read and listen between the lines.
Make Predictions	Crystal Ball	→ Anticipate information to come. → Make logical guesses about what will happen.
Personalize	Me	→ Relate new concepts to your own life, that is, to your experiences, knowledge, beliefs and feelings.
Transfer / Use Cognates	telephone/ telefono/ Telefon/ telefon	→ Apply your linguistic knowledge of other languages (including your native language) to the target language. → Recognize cognates.
Substitute / Paraphrase	Spare Tire	→ Think of a similar word or descriptive phrase for words you do not know in the target language.

Figure 3.1 Learning strategies chart. (continued)
Reprinted with permission from the National Foreign Language Resource Center.

TASK BASED STRATEGIES: USE YOUR IMAGINATION		
Strategy	**Description**	
Use Imagery	Mirror, Mirror	→ Use or create an image to understand and/or represent information.
Use Real Objects / Role Play	Lights, Camera, Action!	→ Act out and/or imagine yourself in different roles in the target language. → Manipulate real objects as you use the target language.

TASK BASED STRATEGIES: USE YOUR ORGANIZATIONAL SKILLS		
Strategy	**Description**	
Find/Apply Patterns	Pattern	→ Apply a rule. → Make a rule. → Sound out and apply letter/sound rules.
Group/Classify	Sort Suits	→ Relate or categorize words or ideas according to attributes.
Use Graphic Organizers/Take Notes	Notepad	→ Use or create visual representations (such as Venn diagrams, time lines, and charts) of important relationships between concepts. → Write down important words and ideas.
Summarize	Main Idea	→ Create a mental, oral, or written summary of information
Use Selective Attention	Look for It	→ Focus on specific information, structures, key words, phrases, or ideas.

Figure 3.1 Learning strategies chart. (continued)
Reprinted with permission from the National Foreign Language Resource Center.

TASK BASED STRATEGIES: USE A VARIETY OF RESOURCES		
Strategy	**Description**	
Access Information Sources		→ Use the dictionary, the internet, and other reference materials.
	Read all about it!	→ Seek out and use sources of information. → Follow a model → Ask questions
Cooperate	Together	Work with others to complete tasks, build confidence, and give and receive feedback.
Talk Yourself Through It (SelfTalk)	I can do it!	Use your inner resources. Reduce your anxiety by reminding yourself of your progress, the resources you have available, and your goals.

Figure 3.1 Learning strategies chart.
Reprinted with permission from the National Foreign Language Resource Center.

board "What was Ben going to buy at the store?" The educator would explain that good readers, in addition to reading the words, always have a little voice in their heads helping them dig deeper into the story's meaning. The words on the page are like lyrics, and what the little voice is saying is like the music. The educator explains that by using these strategies, students will be able to understand more and quickly confront more challenging texts. Students then continue to read, and write their questions on the whiteboards. The educator then gives feedback and other students see everybody's examples.

After a two-week period of repeating this kind of exercise each day with each reading strategy, many students can begin to implement these kinds of strategies on their own. They can begin to demonstrate their use of the strategies in a reading log; see Figure 3.2 for an example of one.

The student projects in this section correlate with California ELD domains 1, 2, 3 4, and 6.

Teaching Others

There are several ways to incorporate students teaching others into classroom practice.

Jigsaw Strategy

One is using the well-known jigsaw strategy. This first entails the teacher dividing one expository text into smaller sections, or identifying multiple expository texts on a similar topic.

READING LOG

SUMMARIZE -- This book/story is about....
PREDICT – I predict that........
ASK QUESTIONS – Will.....?
EVALUATE – I agree/disagree with......   I like/do not like ......
VISUALIZE – Reading "......." makes me see a picture of ....
CONNECT – This makes me remember ....

DATE	BOOK or STORY TITLE	READING STRATEGY USED
3/19/07	The Food We eat	I like the book because I like to eat omelets.
3/20/07	The Food We eat	This makes me remember I and my sister go to the store we eat hamburger and French fries.
3/21/07	Living Together	Makes me see a picture of My family don't have money.
3/22/07	Living Together	This makes me remember My family don't have money and my family don't have oven My family need the compfire.

Figure 3.2   Student reading log example.

Then the teacher makes and distributes several copies of each text to the students—one way is to have students count off by six and give the ones the same text, the twos a different text, and so forth. Another way is to be more strategic in dividing the groups into diverse ethnicities and English proficiency levels. Each student then individually reads the text they have been given along with certain writing/thinking prompts (summarize each paragraph in one sentence; make one connection with the text).

Next, all the students with the same text will meet in a small group and prepare a short oral and poster presentation for the rest of the class teaching the most important elements of the text and sharing some of their responses to the prompts. Then, either that entire group presents to everyone in the class at once, or new groups are formed with one person from each of the first groups, and each person presents to his or her new small group. In either case, the presentations will be made and all listeners take notes and question the presenters.

Teaching Other Classes

Another example is having students teach students in other classes. At the end of a unit (e.g., early North American explorers), students can divide into small groups to prepare very short presentations about different parts of the unit. They then make a poster highlighting parts of the unit they found most interesting, develop an oral presentation involving all members of the group, and prepare related engaging questions to ask their "students." Another class will come in having already been divided into the same number of small groups in the presenting class, and will spend five to seven minutes being taught by each group. Students, then, make a similar presentation five or six times over a 40-minute period of time.

Comic Strips

A third example is one borrowed from Adrian S. Palmer, Theodore S. Rodgers, and Judy Winn-Bell Olsen's excellent book *Back and Forth: Photocopiable Cooperative Pair Activities for Language Development*. That book is composed of reproducible pages designed to develop oral and listening skills in English language learners. In one section, for example, each page has several comic strips, with several frames each. Each frame contains a similar scene, but with some differences (one might have a man throwing a ball to another man on his right, another might have a man throwing a ball to a man on his left, and another might have him kicking the ball). The idea is to have students be in pairs in which one describes a frame in the strip and the other selects the correct one.

A variation on this is after the class has all read the same text for a few days and has built some common vocabulary, students can create their own sheets with their own strips and follow the same process.

The student projects in this section correlate with California ELD domains 1, 2, 3, 4, 5, and 6.

How Can Technology Be Used to Develop Student Leadership?

Technology can be a helpful tool to students as they develop their leadership skills in several ways. New tools beyond the examples shared in this section are constantly being developed.

The Internet is one way to reinforce the freedom of student choice, which helps develop intrinsic motivation. There are hundreds of thousands of online activities that are accessible to English language learners and that promote language development. For example, the Web site set up by Luther Burbank High School teachers (<http://larryferlazzo.com/english.html>) is divided into categories, with many different online exercises in each section. If, for example, you are studying jobs and careers in class, direct students to that section of the Web site, where they can choose from hundreds of activities—all of which reinforce classroom work in different ways.

Computers can also be used to help students feel more comfortable about making mistakes and learning from them. There are thousands of free online activities where students can practice listening, speaking, writing, and reading and get instant feedback—without anyone else seeing their mistakes—on if they are listening, understanding, speaking and writing correctly. This obviously won't eliminate their making errors around others—and, in a relationship-oriented classroom mistakes are celebrated for the risks they entail—but it can build up greater student self-confidence. Appendix 1 shares some of the best of these sites. These include free sites where, if students have a computer microphone available, they can listen to a native English speaker, record it in their own voice as they are reading from the screen, and then have the site instantly assess the accuracy of their pronunciation.

Technology also creates another venue where students can teach and mentor others. Students can help each other play online video games (see chapter 1). Students can also create simple how-to videos or written lessons that can be posted online. These could range from how to make burritos to how best to kick a soccer ball. Again, please see Appendix 1 for further information.

The student projects in this section correlate with California ELD domains 1, 2, 3, 4, 5, and 6.

How Can Student Leadership Development Be Assessed?

The research cited earlier in this chapter shows that reinforcing the qualities of a good language learner/leader—intrinsic motivation, self-efficacy/self-confidence, willingness to take risks and learn from mistakes, and teaching others—is an effective instructional strategy.

For this part of the organizing cycle, as with all the parts, students can again complete an anonymous survey twice a year to help gauge how effective the class has been in developing student leadership.

Here are some questions and a few sample responses:

What qualities do you need to be a leader?

+ Know how to organize, solve problem, not weak and be strong.

+ Responsibility, care for others, wants to help.

+ Listen to other people, understand what they need, fair and fun, be example for other people.

+ Smart and humble.

+ The quality for a leader is power.

+ Be organized and be confident of yourself.

Who are people you think are leaders? Why do you think they are leaders?

- ✦ Teachers, authorities, president, police because they represent us and they have power.
- ✦ Teacher because they have power in class.
- ✦ Cesar Chavez because he did organize.

Do you think you are a leader? Why or why not?

- ✦ I think I am a leader because I help people.
- ✦ I think I am because I help my community.

If you do not think you are a leader, do you want to be one in the future? Why or why not?

- ✦ Yes, I want to be one in the future because that help me feel confident of myself.
- ✦ I think I can be a leader next year because I gained the knowledge to become a leader.
- ✦ In the future I want to be a leader because I want to be more strong.

Have you learned anything in our class this year to help you be a leader? If so, what? And how did you learn it?

- ✦ I have learned a lot doing group activities to make me feel like a leader.
- ✦ Yes, I learned that the leader need to do for help his people and solve the problem.
- ✦ I've done an activity that represents the meaning of a leader. I spoke in front of many people.
- ✦ Learning and helping other people is one of the things I learn this year to be a leader.
- ✦ Yes, I learned about when I feel powerful and learned about how to get a job.

In addition to these biannual evaluations, educators can ask students to periodically write specifically about projects done in class, or respond to questions in an end-of-semester portfolio. For example, after the jobs meeting that was described in the previous chapter, here are some written responses to questions from some of the students who took primary responsibility at that meeting:

How did you feel about your work leading the jobs meeting? Why did you feel that way?

- ✦ I feel good because in that time I had the opportunity to spoke about something that no only help me, but help my community. Also, I feel pride in myself because is not that easy to speak in front to many people.
- ✦ I think I did a really good job. I did what I needed to do with respect. I like it. I felt important and good for being speaking in front of people.

Did you learn anything about yourself from leading the meeting? If you did, what was it?

- ✦ Yes, I learned how to get power . . . When I saw many teachers, parents and friends get together in the meeting, we had more power.
- ✦ I learned that I can speak in front of a lot of people in a microphone and do it well even if is not in my language.

That year, when asked to make a poster and write about their best moment in class, one student drew a large microphone and wrote: "Leading the meeting was my best moment in class because they help me prepare for my leadership quality and I helped make it a great moment by leading the meeting."

After students teach other classes in small groups, here are some sample assessment questions to ask and a few sample responses:

What did you like best about teaching the other class?

✦ The best about teaching other students is *I* feel I done a good job of learning.

✦ I like to teach them what I know.

✦ I like the way that they show us respect by listening and pay attention to us.

✦ I like best about teaching other students because I can learn new things about them.

✦ I like the students ask question about we teaching and we ask question to the students and then the students answer me.

What do you think you did well in your teaching?

✦ I think the thing I did best is I speak loudly and clearly.

✦ We read the words and they understand and know what we say.

What do you think you could have done better?

✦ I could explain more.

✦ Welcome them to this class.

Would you like to do this again? If so, why?

✦ Yes, because when I did this I knew a new thing from other students.

✦ Yes, because it make me try to speak with to other person.

✦ Yes, because they will know what we learn in class.

These examples are representative of the kinds of responses students might write as a result of emphasizing student leadership development. As with the other elements in the organizing cycle, the hope is that after they leave the class, they will not only have developed an appetite for being life-long learners, but also life-long leaders.

What Are the Challenges to Making Student Leadership Development a Priority in the Classroom?

The challenges that face educators here are, like most of the challenges listed in other chapters so far, not necessarily specific to one strategy but are, in fact, ones that teachers have to confront in implementing all parts of the organizing cycle.

Accepting Imperfection

Our students are not going to do a perfect job teaching content and, of course, neither are we. It might be difficult to accept that reality in the moment. However, we need to keep in mind that far more than academic content is being taught and learned at the time of the student teaching. If something is being missed, or incorrectly stated, educators can always clarify it later.

That is not to say that it is okay to let our students fail miserably at their teaching attempts. If a student freezes or is having great difficulties that it does not appear he will overcome on his own relatively quickly, teachers have a responsibility to step in to help. Organizers generally believe that the people they work with don't need help from us to fail—they can do that easily on their own. In fact, most feel that it is far easier to help people (and students) to learn from a difficult situation that you stepped in to help save than it is from a situation where embarrassment and failure occurred.

One key is being aware of that fine line and knowing when a student can recover on his or her own and not jumping in too early to rescue him or her. Another key is to make sure that students are as prepared as they can be for when they teach through role-playing and modeling on the educator's part.

Planning

Abraham Lincoln supposedly said, "Give me six hours to chop down a tree and I will spend the first four sharpening the axe." Yes, planning (sharpening the axe) is essential—student leadership is not going to develop on its own. At the same time, however, you do not want to fall into the trap of paralysis by analysis.

Some efforts at implementing this portion and other parts of the organizing cycle are not going to work out well in the classroom, just as some of our other well-planned typical lessons fall flat. At a certain point we just have to try to learn from our experiences and mistakes, just as good language learners do.

> There is supposedly an ancient Buddhist saying that goes, "You can study the map for years, but you won't get to the village unless you start walking."

Limited by Tradition

Earlier in this chapter, there was a discussion of two types of power—what William Glasser called "power within" and "power with" (which organizers refer to as relational power). There is another kind of power that is often not as positive—Glasser calls it "power over" (Erwin 14), and organizers call it unilateral power. Unilateral power can be exercised by students through destructive acts like cheating or vandalism. Another way it can be exercised over educators (and others) is through the use of custom, habit, and tradition.

> Tradition, or the way we've always done things, can be an impediment to any kind of change. There is a story often told by ministers about a pot roast that illustrates the potential dangers of being limited by some traditions and habits.
> In this story, a husband was watching his wife prepare a pot roast for dinner by cutting it in half. He asked his wife what was the purpose of cutting the meat in half, and his wife replied, "I don't know, but that's how my mother always did it." He then went to the mother, and asked the same question, and received the same response. Finally, he went to the grandmother and asked her the purpose for cutting the roast. She replied, "I didn't have a pan big enough for it to fit in."

Tradition, habit, and custom can clearly have a positive role in our professional and personal lives. But acceptance of it at times can also hold us back. The writer W. Somerset Maugham has a quote attributed to him: "Tradition is a guide, not a jailer."

One writer on community organizing has said that organizing and education have very similar goals. Rene Cardenas writes that the purpose of community development has never been to build a road or improve a park but "to teach others to teach themselves, to learn how to learn, and to evolve from a history of dependence . . . to one of independence and helpfulness" (Colombo 34).

This connection could be no clearer than in the goal of developing leadership ability in our students.

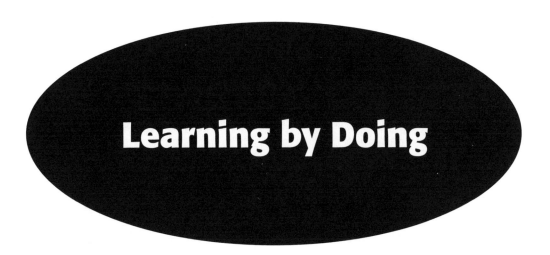

CHAPTER 4

Learning by Doing

The class of beginning English language learners had been learning money-related vocabulary and had written about some pictures. They had also just begun learning basic verbs. I had taken a few correctly written and a few incorrectly written sentences and copied them on a transparency in two columns, which you can see in Figure 4.1.

Keeping most of the sheet covered, I showed students and read aloud the first example listed under "Yes"—"One dollar is equal to four quarters"—and then did the same for the one under "No"—"Four nickels is equal to twenty pennies." Everybody in the room stared intently at the screen. I asked them to think silently for a minute and try to figure out if they knew why one was "yes" (correct) and one was "no" (incorrect). I then asked them to share what they thought with a neighbor, and asked if anybody knew why. Though there had been a lot of animated discussion, no one hazarded a guess.

I then moved the sheet covering the rest of the examples down further and showed and read the next two examples, and asked students again to think and share if they had any idea why one column was "yes" and the other "no." By then, eight hands came up and all eight had figured out the verb should be plural—and why it was plural—in the incorrect sentences.

I handed out small whiteboards and asked students to write down how they would correctly write the sentences under the "No" column. As they would lift up their boards, I would tell them if they had rewritten the sentences correctly—everyone in the class had. At that point, I called on students to come up to the overhead projector to correctly rewrite the sentences for all to see.

CONCEPT ATTAINMENT EXAMPLE

<u>YES</u>	<u>NO</u>
One dollar is equal to four quarters.	
	Four nickels is equal to twenty pennies.
One quarter is equal to two dimes and one nickel.	
	Two dollars is equal to two hundred pennies.
Five dimes are equal to two quarters.	
	Two nickels is equal to one dime.
Five pennies are equal to one nickel.	
	Two quarters is equal to five dimes.

Figure 4.1   Concept attainment example.

Finally, I asked students to write on their whiteboards in their own words how they could determine if they should use "is" or "are" in a sentence. "1 = is, Many = are" was typical of what students wrote.

Students had been introduced briefly to a concept prior to this lesson. Then, using the guided induction strategy called "concept attainment," they began to gain proficiency by constructing their own knowledge. They solved a puzzle that was based on their own work (including errors), and then everyone in the class had to individually reinforce their newfound knowledge. The teacher was able to check for understanding with each student. Students then summarized the concept they had learned.

What Do You Mean by Learning by Doing?

The phrase "learning by doing" was popularized by education theorist and philosopher John Dewey. It generally means that students (and, in fact, anyone) can learn more from the experience of solving problems on their own instead of just being told how to do it. He explained it this way: "When we experience something, we act upon it, we do something with it; then we suffer or undergo the consequence. We do something to the thing and then it does something to us in return" (Dewey 139).

Dewey, however, in his later years, grew frustrated by how his perspective had been misinterpreted: "I don't believe people learn by merely doing. The important things are the ideas that a man puts into his doing. Unintelligent doing will result in his doing the wrong thing" (Haroutunian-Gordon 477). Dewey felt it was important to "keep the experience of the student moving in the direction of what the expert already knows" (Dewey 184).

Dewey's disdain for a romantic vision of how people learn is echoed in a similar perspective shared by community organizers. Organizers commonly refer to this kind of experiential learning as learning through actions (which happens to come from the Latin word "agere," which means "to do, stir up"). In organizing, these actions can be any kind of planned activity—either individual or collective. And, just as some educators miss Dewey's emphasis on providing guidance, some organizers make the same mistake. Most organizers, however, keep in mind an old organizing dictum: People don't need our help to fail—they can do that quite well on their own. These organizers strike a balance between allowing people to learn by doing on their own and providing structure and advice. Failure rarely motivates.

An additional important point to keep in mind is the organizing perspective that the action is in the reaction. In other words, it is not sufficient to say that you taught it. The real question is: Was it learned?

The underpinning of this kind of learning perspective is best expressed by a quote attributed to Confucius: "I hear and I forget. I see and I remember. I do and I understand."

More recently, this idea of learning by doing has been framed as a learner-centered classroom. Specific elements of this kind of environment include inductive methods (similar to the opening story in this chapter) and problem-based learning (<http://www.glencoe.com/sec/teaching today/subject/creating_learn_centered.phtml>). Stephen Krashen's concept of free voluntary reading can also be considered another element.

A final quote to consider in understanding this concept is attributed to longtime Columbia University professor, poet, and writer Mark van Doren, who said, "The art of teaching is the art of assisting discovery."

What Does Research Say about Learning by Doing?

This chapter will focus on three specific examples of learning by doing:

✦ Inductive teaching

✦ Problem-based learning

✦ Free voluntary reading

Inductive Teaching

Teaching *inductively* generally means providing students with a number of examples from which they can create a pattern and form a concept or rule. It utilizes Jerome Bruner's definition of knowledge as the ability to "derive the unknown from the known" (Bruner, *The Culture of Education* 51). Teaching *deductively* is first providing the rule or concept and then having students practice applying it.

Research in Action—Teaching and Learning Inductively

For a unit on the meaning of signs, small groups of students were given cameras to take pictures of signs around the school and in the neighborhood on a field trip. After the pictures were printed, group members helped each other learn their meaning and put their photos into categories they determined. In addition, they had to explain in writing what clues they used to decide which sign belonged in which category. Most groups came up with categories like "Warning," "Names," "Give Directions." Students shared their conclusions and challenged each other if they disagreed.

Research on how the brain learns has concluded that our brains find meaning through searching for patterns. As Judy Willis, neurologist, teacher, and author, has written:

> Education is about increasing the patterns that students can use, recognize, and communicate. As the ability to see and work with patterns expands, the executive functions are enhanced. Whenever new material is presented in such a way that students see relationships, they generate greater brain cell activity (forming new neural connections) and achieve more successful long-term memory storage and retrieval. (Willis 15)

Renate Nummela Caine and Geoffrey Caine elaborate on this particular brain processing phenomenon: "Although we choose much of what students are to learn, the ideal process is to present the information in a way that allows brains to extract patterns, rather than attempt to impose them" (Caine and Caine 89).

A number of studies have specifically demonstrated the effectiveness of the inductive model. In one, fourth-graders used

> the inductive model to . . . explore the techniques used by published authors to accomplish tasks such as announcing the main idea clearly, introducing characters, establishing setting, and describing actions. The students, having characterized several devices that authors use for accomplishing similar tasks, then experimented with those devices in their own writing . . . Their end-of-year scores for writing quality were higher than the end-of-year scores for eighth grade students the previous year! (Joyce and Calhoun 176)

Another study compared two groups of 10th graders studying a botany unit. One group used an inductive strategy, while the other used the textbook. Scores in the inductive model group were approximately 30 percent higher than in the control group (Joyce and Calhoun 178). A study comparing inductive and deductive models in a second language classroom for French learners showed that grammar quiz scores were "significantly greater" for those in the inductive group (Haight, Herron, and Cole 296).

Problem-Based Learning

Problem-based learning generally has several characteristics, including: it's often done in a small group of students, they are investigating an open-ended question, and the teacher is more of a facilitator than a sage-on-stage (<http://www.glencoe.com/sec/teachingtoday/subject/creating_learn_centered.phtml>).

Research in Action—Problem-Based Learning

Students were divided into pairs and were given two empty plastic cups, scissors, and one cup filled with water. The educator told students to see if they could figure out a way to tell time using those three items. After awhile, most groups identified some version of how ancient Greeks did it—by poking a hole in the bottom of one cup and pouring water through it so it fell into the other cup. Two of the groups also determined the water would fall in a different rate depending on the size of the hole.

The educator then asked students to draw and write out the steps that they took from the beginning of their work to the end. After they were done, the educator introduced the vocabulary of the scientific method (*hypothesis, predict, experiment, test, conclusion,* etc.), and students used their newly learned words to label their steps. Later, there was a class discussion about other times outside of science the scientific method might be used to learn something—where they began with a hypothesis, tried an experiment, learned it didn't work, and tried something differently until they figured it out. Students shared many other examples, including shooting a basketball and baking a cake. Students then made posters showing when they had used the scientific method in their own lives and labeled each step using the new academic vocabulary words.

A number of studies have demonstrated the effectiveness of problem-based learning. A three-year study compared math students at one British school using problem-based learning and those at another school using a more traditional method. In a study designed by Jo Boaler, three times as many students from the problem-based learning school passed the national math exam.

In Mergendoller, Maxwell, and Bellisimo's study covering teachers at four different California high schools, students in economics classes using the problem-based learning approach scored higher in assessments than those in traditional classes. Science students using problem-based learning in another study scored 13 percent higher in standardized tests than those in traditional classes, and elementary school students in classes using the same instructional method scored higher in reading assessments than those in other schools (Hmelo-Silver, Duncan, and Chinn 104).

Though there appear to be no comparative studies specifically examining problem-based learning and second language learning, researchers consider these kinds of group collaboration for problem solving superior opportunities for language acquisition (Mathews-Aydinli 5).

Free Voluntary Reading

Free voluntary reading means that students can read what they want without an expectation that they will have to report or answer questions on what they have read. This popular strategy, which in class is sometimes called silent sustained reading (SSR), has been extensively researched and found to be effective at increasing student reading achievement (<http://www.sdcoe.k12.ca.us/score/promising/tips/tipfvr.html>).

In addition, according to Stephen Krashen's "Applying the Comprehension Hypothesis," recent studies "consistently report a positive relationship between the amount of free reading done and various aspects of second and foreign language competence when the amount of formal instruction students had is statistically controlled" (1).

Tech Tip—Accessing High-Interest Reading Materials

There are tens of thousands of free fiction and expository text resources online that are accessible to English language learners. Starfall (<http://www.starfall.com/>) and Literactive (<http://www.literactive.com/Home/index.asp>) are just two among many that are listed in Appendix 1. These Web sites usually provide audio support for the text and often highlight each word as they are pronounced. In addition, many have images that reinforce meaning. This support is especially valuable in engaging older English language learner students. Technology lets them more quickly access higher level text than the ABC texts designed for very young children.

What Are Examples of Learning by Doing in the Classroom?

A number of the lesson ideas shared in previous chapters could also fit here, and, even in this section, many elements of a learner-centered classroom flow into one another. These lesson ideas will be described by highlighting how they correspond with one of the three learning by doing strategies—the inductive model, problem-based learning, or free voluntary learning.

Inductive Model

Picture Word Inductive Model

The picture word inductive model (PWIM) is a strategy that has been shown to be effective in teaching beginning readers, including second-language learners (Calhoun, Poirier, Simon, and Mueller 8).

Emily Calhoun originally developed this instructional method and wrote about it in her book, *Teaching Beginning Reading and Writing With the Picture Word Inductive Model.* There are various ways to implement it in the classroom, and the PWIM unit plan is one adaptation for English language learners.

Picture Word Inductive Model Unit Plan

Instructional Objectives

Students will:

1. Learn at least 20 new theme-related vocabulary words.
2. Develop categorization skills.
3. Write an essay.

Duration

Five approximately 35-minute lessons over a five-day period.

English Language Development Standards: California English Language Development (ELD) Domains

1. Students use English for everyday communication in socially and culturally appropriate ways and apply listening and speaking skills and strategies in the classroom.
2. Students apply word analysis skills and knowledge of vocabulary to read fluently.
5. Students will write well-organized, clear, and coherent text in a variety of academic genres.
6. Students will apply the conventions of standard English usage orally and in writing.

Materials

1. Enlarged laminated photo representative of a thematic unit (food, sports, school, etc.) mounted on poster board with border space around the image. The photo should reflect a real-life incident, and should have multiple different objects.
2. A copy of the photo for each student (photocopied).

3. A data set composed of a list of sentences about the picture with blanks in them. Potential answers are below each sentence. Copies for each student. (See Figure 4.2 for an example.)

Procedure

First Day

1. Teacher asks all students to come to the front of the room and stand in front of the laminated picture. He asks if students can say in English what some of the things are that they see. As students say a word and point to it in the picture, the teacher writes each letter, asking students to repeat it, and then says the word—again asking students to repeat. He then draws an arrow from the word to the object. This process should continue until there are approximately 20 words on the photo, including new words that the teacher has added.

2. Students then return to their seats and copy the words in the same way on their individual photos.

3. Teacher reviews the words again.

4. After class, the teacher develops a data set of sentences about the picture using all the words that were labeled.

Second Day

1. Teacher reviews the words on the image, asking students to repeat.

2. Students are asked to put the words into three or four categories on a sheet of paper, leaving space for additions. Then can work individually or in pairs. If students have not done this before, preface this activity with the introduction to categories exercise in the "I feel powerful . . ." lesson plan.

3. After a few minutes, the teacher will ask students to share a few of the category names they have identified and write them on the board (e.g., words that start with "p," people-related words, things that are red). This is to help students who are having a difficult time categorizing. A few minutes later, the teacher will ask one or two students he has identified to share one list of words they have categorized—without saying the name of the category. He will then ask students to think for a moment—without saying anything—what category those words might be in. He will next ask students to share their answers with a partner and then call on students to share their guesses. After each time a student says what he or she thinks it is, the teacher will ask the student who gave the words if it is correct or not.

4. Next, the teacher will ask students to use their dictionaries and prior knowledge to add three or four new words to their categories.

5. Students share—orally and in writing—with a partner their completed work.

Third Day

1. Teacher reviews the words on the image, asking students to repeat.

2. Teacher distributes a data set composed of a list of sentences with blanks in them. Potential answers are below each sentence.

3. Students fill in the blanks and then share—both orally and in writing—their answers with a partner.

4. Teacher reviews the answers with the class.

FOOD PICTURE SENTENCES

1. The family is sitting at the _____. There is a _____ on the table.

   travel   tablecloth   lunch   table

2. There are three _____ and two _____ on the table.

   forks   spoons   knives   plates

3. The woman is wearing a _____ shirt. The man and the woman are wearing _____.

   eyeglasses   black   red   smile

4. The girl is eating _____ with her _____.

   fruit   hands   vegetables   meat

5. We know the family is _____ because they are _____.

   sad   frown   smiling   happy

6. There are _____ in a _____ on the table.

   pizza   bowl   plate   strawberries

7. The girl eating meat has a _____. No one else has a napkin. They don't need one because they _____ before.

   ate   glass   cup   napkin

8. There are two _____ on the table. There is nothing in them. They are _____.

   plates   empty   glasses   people

9. There is a white _____ on the _____.

   curtain   window   person   car

10. There are _____ inside the window and _____ outside the window

    pears   trees   plants   pigs

Figure 4.2 Cloze example for picture word inductive model.

5. Teacher asks the students to put the sentences into at least three categories (either by cutting and pasting each sentence under the name of a category or by writing the name of a category and underneath writing the numbers of the sentences that belong there). The teacher can provide the categories or ask students to develop their own. A similar process to step number three in the previous day is then done. Students must also underline the clue words they used to determine whether the sentence belongs in that particular category.

6. Students then write three additional sentences about the picture under each category either in class or as homework.

Fourth Day

1. Teacher reviews the words on the image, asking students to repeat.

2. Teacher asks students to rewrite their categories as paragraphs, explaining some of the structure of an essay (indent paragraphs, a single line between them, etc.).

Fifth Day

1. Teacher reviews the words on the image.

2. Teacher asks students to develop titles for their essays. Student share their titles and they are all written on easel paper next to the laminated photo.

3. Essays are turned in and student writing is used for lessons using concept attainment (see first story at the beginning of the chapter) in the following days.

Assessment

1. Teacher gives test including all 20 words. Teacher says the word, uses it in a sentence, then says the word again. The test also includes completing sentences with blanks, sentence scrambles (mixing up the words in a sentence and asking students to reorder them correctly), and other items covered during the week.

2. Students exchange papers with each other for checking as the teacher says the correct answer, or asks students to contribute them. Students are told to put check marks next to the answers that are correct. Papers are returned to students and then given to teacher for review.

Possible Extensions/Modifications

1. After the second day, the teacher could have students lead the class in reviewing the words at the beginning of the lesson.

2. Depending on the class level, more sophisticated writing elements (topic sentence, thesis statement, etc.) can be taught and used.

3. Depending on the class level, students could label the laminated photo with sentences they generate the first day, which can also be used in the data set.

A unit plan like this could be used as a regular feature in class—perhaps starting on Monday and finishing on a Friday. Other activities and exercises connected to the picture's theme could be organized during the same period of time. The images used could include students or be taken from field trips. If one week's topic was going to be kitchen-related vocabulary, a camera or two could be shared so each student could label a picture of their own kitchen. By the end of the school year, there could be 20 or 30 large photos on the classroom walls with labeled vocabulary that would be ideal for constant reinforcement activities, including games (see Appendix 2).

Inductive Data Sets

"Data set" is the term used to describe a list of words, sentences, paragraphs, or pictures that students are asked to put into categories. Students developed their own data sets in the "I feel powerful when . . ." lesson plan and in the pictures of signs described earlier in this chapter. The teacher created the one-sentence clozes (Figure 4.2) used in the PWIM lesson. In some cases, especially when students are first introduced to the concept, it may be best for teachers to suggest categories. Later, as students become more familiar with the inductive model, they can create their own.

Tech Tip–Creating Picture Data Sets Online

Students can create their own data sets online by using categories they've already used in the classroom or inventing their own on the topic the class is studying. By grabbing images off the Web (see Appendix 1 for a discussion on legal issues) or uploading their own photos, they can write a one-sentence description of each image and place them in categories on a student/teacher blog or Web site. In addition, they can mix up their images, list the names of categories, and have other students try to organize them.

Data sets can be used to study any topic in any subject. A science class studying buoyancy could have students bring in a number of different objects to test if they would float or not and be able to categorize those that did and those that did not. The data set in Figure 4.3 is an example of using data sets to help teach reading strategies. Using lessons structured in a similar way to the ones shared previously, students can share their conclusions and justifications, and add their own examples to categories.

Classroom Story–Learning Phonics Inductively

I distribute a sheet with a series of pictures that would be described by words containing the long A sounds. Some use "ai" and some just include the letter "a" and "silent e at the end" patterns. It's easy to make your own, but I use purchased reproducibles from Sharron Bassano's book, *Sounds Easy!* Each picture has one or two of the letters in the descriptive word missing. I have the same sheet on the overhead, and I call out the number of the picture and say the word, giving students a few moments to fill in each blank letter with what they think it is before I write it out on the transparency.

After we've completed the sheet and reviewed them again together, students pair up and quickly practice pronouncing the words. They then work together to put the words into two or three categories. They could be words that have "ai," words that have just "a" with a silent "e" at the end, or categories that reflect how they're used—food, for example. Pairs then become groups of four, comparing their categories and deciding if they want to keep the ones they have or if they like the ones the other pair created. Using dictionaries, and the Internet if computers are available, students

READING STRATEGIES DATA SET

Put these examples into these categories: **Summarize, Predict, Ask Questions, Evaluate, Visualize, and Connect**

1. This story is about a girl's first day at school. She is afraid when she goes into class, but she has fun.

2. Will Jane go out with John or Jeff?

3. I disagree with Dia's decision to marry Tou.

4. Reading "he was shot" makes me see a picture of a man falling down.

5. This part of the story makes me remember the movie I saw about planets.

6. This part of the story makes me remember another story I read about the weather.

7. I predict that the tiger will eat the children because he is hungry.

8. I agree with the father's decision to not let his daughter go out with Toua.

9. I disagree with the boy's decision to go into the woods.

10. Will the family get out before the flood comes?

11. Will the girl buy the SUV or the small car?

12. I predict the girl will buy the small car because it is cheaper.

13. This part of the story tells about the family's trip to America. It was long and hard.

14. The problem that John has in the story makes me remember when I had the same problem.

15. The title of the book is *Sports*. I predict it will tell about basketball, football, soccer, and baseball.

16. This makes me remember when my uncle died.

17. Will the boy live or die when the car crashes?

18. Reading "it was snowing" makes me see a picture of snowflakes, children throwing snowballs, and snowmen.

Figure 4.3   Reading strategies data set.
From *English Language Learners: Teaching Strategies that Work* by Larry Ferlazzo. Santa Barbara, CA: Linworth. Copyright © 2010.

then add words into their categories. The groups create posters of their categories and determine two or three important lessons they have learned, which they present to the entire class the next day.

> All of them concluded that the letter "a" was pronounced with a "long" sound if it appeared as an "ai" or if it was the third letter from the end of a word that ended with an "e."

The student projects in this section correlate with California ELD domains 1, 2, 5, and 6.

Implementing Problem-Based Learning
What Neighborhood Do You Want to Live In?

A unit designed for students to decide what kind of neighborhood they wanted to live in was used with a class of beginning English language learners to help them learn "city"-related vocabulary and develop basic descriptive writing skills. The same unit was used with an intermediate English class preparing to write a persuasive essay.

The unit began with a teacher-prepared survey titled "Important Qualities in a Neighborhood." The survey was framed in a way to highlight the *assets* (diversity, mass transit) found in the school's community. Students rated each quality on a 1–3 scale, added other things they'd like to see in a neighborhood, and justified their decisions in writing. Students then met in small groups to share their ratings and change them if they wanted to after the discussion. See Figure 4.4 for an example of the survey form.

Students next went on two field trips—one a walking tour of the neighborhood around the school, and the other a similar visit to one of the richest neighborhoods in the city—the so-called Fabulous 40s. In small groups, they took pictures and completed a checklist noting what they saw. The checklist is presented in Figure 4.5. Next, students did a statistical and demographic analysis of each neighborhood using Web applications accessible to beginning English language learners.

Tech Tip—Neighborhood Analyses

There are numerous free and easy-to-use Web tools useful for researching specific neighborhoods. These include sites like ZipSkinny (<http://zipskinny.com/>), which will provide you up-to-date U.S. Census data by ZIP code; Walk Score (<http://www.walkscore.com/>), designed to rate how easy it is to walk to important services from specific addresses; and Housing Mapper (http://www.housingmaps.com/), which shows the price of homes and apartments for rent or sale in different communities. More sites can be found in Appendix 1.

Students then wrote about the neighborhoods and illustrated their essays with the photos they took. Most preferred their own neighborhood over the Fabulous 40s:

Veronica wrote, "I like this neighborhood because railroad near by my house and I can easily travel by train; and I like it because I love Russian food and I can easily buy them in Russian store . . . Also I like it because there's my church with my friends and relations.

IMPORTANT QUALITIES IN A NEIGHBORHOOD

Rate each quality: 1 = Not Important

2 = A Little Important

3 = Very Important

Write a sentence explaining why you gave it that rating
(Example: If you rated "Parks are nearby" as a "3" you could write: I gave this a 3 because my family goes to play in parks a lot.)

You may add other qualities.

1. Ethnic diversity _____

2. Easy to get to places by bus or light rail _____

3. Housing is affordable _____

4. Churches are nearby _____

5. Parks are nearby _____

6. Stores are nearby _____

7. Schools are nearby _____

8. Many people who share your ethnicity live in the neighborhood _____

9. Grocery stores that sell your ethnic food are nearby. _____

10.

11.

Figure 4.4   Neighborhood qualities survey.
From *English Language Learners: Teaching Strategies that Work* by Larry Ferlazzo. Santa Barbara, CA: Linworth. Copyright © 2010.

Neighborhood Field Trip Checklist:

Name: _____

Burbank neighborhood	Fabulous 40's
Places where people live: Check every time you see: A house _____ A duplex _____ An apartment _____ A trailer or trailer park _____	**Places where people live:** Check every time you see: A house _____ A duplex _____ An apartment _____ A trailer or trailer park _____
Pick one house and answer these questions: Is this house: big _____, medium _____, small _____- Does it have a fence around it? Yes _____ No _____ Chain link _____ Wood _____ Other kind offence _____ How many windows does it have? _____ Are the windows barred? _____ What do you like about this house?	Pick one house and answer these questions: Is this house: big _____, medium _____, small _____- Does it have a fence around it? Yes _____ No _____ Chain link _____ Wood _____ Other kind of fence _____ How many windows does it have? _____ Are the windows barred? _____ What do you like about this house?
Commercial places: Check when you see A food store _____ An ethnic food store _____ A clothes store _____ A restaurant _____ A health service _____	Commercial places: Check when you see A food store _____ An ethnic food store _____ A clothes store _____ A restaurant _____ A health service _____
Other commercial: What do you see that you like?	Other commercial: What do you see that you like?
Check when you see: A bus stop _____ Light rail _____	Check when you see: A bus stop _____ Light rail _____

Figure 4.5   Neighborhood checklist.

From *English Language Learners: Teaching Strategies that Work* by Larry Ferlazzo. Santa Barbara, CA: Linworth. Copyright © 2010.

Nayeli didn't like the Fabulous 40s: "I don't like it because there's not many variety of race and people and the houses are expensive."

Students then designed their ideal neighborhood, described it, and explained why they made their choices. Finally, they presented their neighborhoods in small groups to students from other classes and graded themselves using a simple rubric:

1. Did you only speak English?

2. Did you introduce yourself and ask the other students' names?

3. Did you use the index card notes you wrote?

4. Did you look at the other people when you spoke?

5. Did you ask what they would like to see in their ideal neighborhoods?

U.S. Citizenship

Over a period of two months the class had been concentrating on two different threads related to U.S. citizenship. One concentrated on preparation for the official test—students studied the workbook, practiced dictation, and used online activities for reinforcement. The other explored what an active citizen might look like. This primarily included students doing the individual meetings and organizing the public forum with job training agencies that was discussed in the previous chapter.

Then the class reviewed the different activities that were done for each of the two threads and completed a graphic organizer, which is shown in Figure 4.6. Next, the class brainstormed answers to the following questions:

✦ What is a good citizen?

✦ What does a good citizen know?

✦ What does a good citizen do?

Finally, each student wrote which thread they thought helped prepare them the most to become what they defined as a good citizen and why. Students had different perspectives:

✦ Toua: "A good citizen is someone who know about their native history, good helper, work hard, and know about the laws in their country . . . I think studying for the citizenship test help me prepare to be a good citizen more than community organizing because when you learn about the constitution and history you might be a good citizen and leader."

✦ Pao: "A good citizen is someone who helps the community and makes the community better . . . I think community organizing helped me prepare to be a good citizen more than studying for the citizenship text because I learn how to solve the community's problems and I know how to help the community."

✦ Chi: "A good citizen is someone who know a lot about country and history . . . I think being an active citizen and community organizing helped me prepare to be a good citizen more than studying for the citizen test because it helped me know my family member, friends, neighbors, jobs and learned about power."

Which Helped You Become a Better Citizen?

List the different activities we did.

Studying for the citizenship test	Being an active citizen and community organizing

Write a paragraph about your experience.

First, begin your paragraph with "A good citizen is someone who. . ."

Second, list three activities we did studying for the citizenship test and tell how they helped you.

Third, list three activities we did learning how to be active citizens and community organizers and tell how they helped you.

Finally, write which helped you more, studying for the test, or active citizens and community organizing, tell why. "I think _____ helped me prepare to be a good citizen more than _____, this is because . . ."

Figure 4.6   Student citizenship project example (developed by Elisabeth Belan).
From *English Language Learners: Teaching Strategies that Work* by Larry Ferlazzo. Santa Barbara, CA: Linworth. Copyright © 2010.

◆ Mai Tong: "A good citizen is someone who knows about governments and history . . . I think active citizen and community organizing helped me be a good citizen more than studying for the test, this is because a good citizen need to know how to organize and have community service. This also help me to practice speak English for many people and feel confident."

The student projects in this section correlate California ELD domains 1, 2, 3, 5, and 6.

Implementing Free Voluntary Reading

A simple way to implement free voluntary reading in the classroom is to begin each day with 15 minutes of students reading whatever books they want. A critical component of a successful reading program is to have a large selection of high-interest accessible resources in your classroom and school library. A school librarian can be a key ally in identifying and obtaining good books, especially ones for older English language learners who would rather not be reading books designed for young children.

Tech Tip—Printable Books Online

There are many online resources of accessible short books with high-interest content that can easily be downloaded and printed out (see Appendix 1 for details). Many are free, though one of the best, Reading A-Z (<http://www.readinga-z.com/>), is only available by a paid subscription. For $80 per year, teachers can download hundreds of accessible short fiction and nonfiction books.

Though this kind of reading in class is typically done silently, having two or three English language learners read the same book quietly together can be a useful language-development activity as they can help each other with decoding, pronunciation, and meaning. During this 15-minute period, the educator can be checking in with students, having individuals read a paragraph aloud to him, helping others find a good book, and assisting those with questions. School librarians can assist in student visits to their facility, and a field trip to the public library can also be part of this reading effort.

Even though the idea of free voluntary reading typically discourages much in the way of formal reporting from students, it does not preclude students from acting the way most of us do when we are reading a good book—telling somebody about it. For example, there could be weekly book talks of a few minutes each during which students break into pairs or larger groups and share what their books are about, what they like about them, and perhaps read a quote that they like.

Students can also be asked to read a book of their choice at home for 30 minutes each night—with or without a formal accountability system of a reading log (like the one in Figure 3.2) or a parent signature form. Time can also be spent in the computer lab at school—or on the computer at home if one is available—accessing the reading sites listed in Appendix 1.

The student projects in this section correlate with California ELD domains 1, 2, 3, 4, and 6.

How Can Technology Be Used to Reinforce Learning by Doing?

In addition to the ideas already shared in this chapter's "Tech Tips," there are numerous other ways for technology to provide a value-added benefit to student learning by doing. Many methods could particularly reflect work done in problem-based learning efforts and expand on student free voluntary learning.

Webquests and Internet Scavenger Hunts

Webquests are online projects that require students to use a variety of teacher-suggested Web sites to accomplish a challenging task that often involves answering a question. For example, researching and deciding the best car to purchase; determining if wolves should be reintroduced to Yellowstone National Park; or exploring and concluding whether Alexander Graham Bell was the true inventor of the telephone. Teachers First (<http://www.teachersfirst.com/summer/webquest/quest-b.shtml>) has a good overview on how to create a Webquest, and additional resources can be found in Appendix 1. Students can also create their own for others to complete—either for their classmates or for placement on a site like Zunal (<http://www.zunal.com/>), which hosts teacher-and-student–developed Webquests and scavenger hunts.

Internet scavenger hunts are a much simpler use of the Web and can function as an engaging tool for students to learn content. They typically consist of a series of questions associated to a different Web pages where students can find the answers. Again, resources for scavenger hunt creation are in Appendix 1.

Authentic Audience

One of the main opportunities the Web provides is a place for students to create academic work that will actually have an authentic audience outside the classroom. Knowing that their creations will be in full public view and seen and used by others throughout the world can help students motivate themselves to work at their full potential. More ideas can be found in Appendix 1, but a few are presented in the following sections.

Make a Travel Guide

Ruba (<http://www.ruba.com/>) and Next Step (<http://www.nextstop.com/>) are just two of many sites where it's possible to write guides to places where you have visited or where you live and say what you like or don't like—and why. For example, small groups could respond to the question: "If a visitor only has three days to spend seeing your city, how should he or she spend it and why?"

Research Companies

Project Label (<https://projectlabel.org/index.php>) is a site that collects research anyone does on the social nutrition (safety, environmental impact, nutritional value of products, etc.) of companies. Student small groups, for example, could research companies that have a local presence to contribute data to the site and determine if it is important to take those issues into consideration before using a company's products and, if so, which ones should they recommend to their families and friends to use and why.

Create a How-to Video

Graspr (<http://www.graspr.com/>) and Monkey See (<http://www.monkeysee.com/>) are two student-friendly sites where students can upload instructional videos they create. Small student groups could decide on a skill they want to teach, and explore answers to the question, "What are the steps one needs to go through to effectively teach a skill?"

Develop a Top 10 List

Students can make a top 10 list of anything they want—cars, books, video games—and describe the reasons for their rankings. Two popular sites that encourage user contributions (and make it easy to do so) are Lists of Bests (<http://www.listsofbests.com/>) and The Top Tens (<http://www.the-top-tens.com/>). As in the travel guide exercise, student groups could consider, for example, what criteria they would deem important in deciding what kind of car to purchase and then research those elements to develop a top 10 list of appropriate cars. Justifications for the rankings can be included.

Design and Create an Online Book

In addition to implementing free voluntary reading by viewing online fiction and nonfiction books that provide audio and visual support for the text, students can create their own books for others to read at free sites like Tar Heel Reader (<http://tarheelreader.org/>) and Tikatok (<http://www.tikatok.com/>).

The student projects in this section correlate with California ELD domains 1, 2, 3, 5, and 6.

How Do You Assess Learning by Doing?

The research cited in this chapter demonstrates that the learning by doing strategies discussed here are effective in raising student achievement levels. There are several ways that a teacher can determine their effectiveness in her own classroom.

Teaching Inductively

Though standardized test scores are considered a limited evaluative tool by some, they are one that are used by schools and can help assess the effectiveness of instructional strategies. In Sacramento, California, most of Luther Burbank High School's mainstream ninth-grade English classes and many of its social studies classes are taught using an inductive curriculum from Pebble Creek Labs (<http://pebblecreeklabs.com/>). Rising test scores in 2008 allowed Burbank to exit Fourth Year Program Improvement Status under the No Child Left Behind Act (Zehr 1).

Having students create their own inductive unit on a topic of their choice, and then teach a small portion of it to the class, is one way to assess if students have grasped the inductive method and are better prepared to use this process of discovery in their lifelong learning.

Various kinds of anonymous surveys, including the sample one in Figure 4.7, can also be used as an assessment tool. Note that in that survey, students are asked to rate the same activity twice—first by how much they liked it and second by how helpful it was to their learning.

ENGLISH CLASS SURVEY

1. Please rate how much you liked these activities. "1" means you hated it and "10" means you loved it:

* Reading in class	1	2	3	4	5	6	7	8	9	10
* Introductions	1	2	3	4	5	6	7	8	9	10
* Science experiments	1	2	3	4	5	6	7	8	9	10
* Computer	1	2	3	4	5	6	7	8	9	10
* English chants	1	2	3	4	5	6	7	8	9	10
* Songs	1	2	3	4	5	6	7	8	9	10
* Pictures and paragraphs	1	2	3	4	5	6	7	8	9	10
* Writing a story	1	2	3	4	5	6	7	8	9	10
* Reading at home	1	2	3	4	5	6	7	8	9	10
* Letter sounds	1	2	3	4	5	6	7	8	9	10
* Personal dictionary	1	2	3	4	5	6	7	8	9	10
* Games	1	2	3	4	5	6	7	8	9	10
* Field trips and scavenger hunts	1	2	3	4	5	6	7	8	9	10
* Watching videos and writing about them	1	2	3	4	5	6	7	8	9	10

2. Please rate how much you *learned* from these activities. "1" means you did not learn much from it and "10" means you learned a lot from it.

* Reading in class	1	2	3	4	5	6	7	8	9	10
* Introductions	1	2	3	4	5	6	7	8	9	10
* Science experiments	1	2	3	4	5	6	7	8	9	10
* Computer	1	2	3	4	5	6	7	8	9	10

Figure 4.7 Student class survey. (continued)
From *English Language Learners: Teaching Strategies that Work* by Larry Ferlazzo. Santa Barbara, CA: Linworth. Copyright © 2010.

* English chants	1	2	3	4	5	6	7	8	9	10
* Songs	1	2	3	4	5	6	7	8	9	10
* Pictures and paragraphs	1	2	3	4	5	6	7	8	9	10
* Writing a story	1	2	3	4	5	6	7	8	9	10
* Reading at home	1	2	3	4	5	6	7	8	9	10
* Letter sounds	1	2	3	4	5	6	7	8	9	10
* Personal dictionary	1	2	3	4	5	6	7	8	9	10
* Games	1	2	3	4	5	6	7	8	9	10
* Field trips and scavenger hunts	1	2	3	4	5	6	7	8	9	10
* Watching videos and writing about them	1	2	3	4	5	6	7	8	9	10

3. Please rate Mr. Ferlazzo. "1" is the lowest grade and "10" is the highest:

* Patience	1	2	3	4	5	6	7	8	9	10
* Getting to know students	1	2	3	4	5	6	7	8	9	10
* Friendly	1	2	3	4	5	6	7	8	9	10
* Class discipline	1	2	3	4	5	6	7	8	9	10
* Fair	1	2	3	4	5	6	7	8	9	10
* Knows what he is doing	1	2	3	4	5	6	7	8	9	10
* Is organized and prepared	1	2	3	4	5	6	7	8	9	10
* Works hard	1	2	3	4	5	6	7	8	9	10
* Talks too much	1	2	3	4	5	6	7	8	9	10

4. How do you feel about having Mr. Ferlazzo as a teacher again? "1" means you hate it and "10" means you are very happy about it.

	1	2	3	4	5	6	7	8	9	10

5. The pace of this class is:

Too slow   Just right   Too fast

Figure 4.7   Student class survey. (continued)
From *English Language Learners: Teaching Strategies that Work* by Larry Ferlazzo. Santa Barbara, CA: Linworth. Copyright © 2010.

6. I think the class would be better if we . . .

- studied more grammar   _____

- used the textbook more   _____

- worked on speaking English more _____

- other _____

_____

_____

Figure 4.7   Student class survey.
From *English Language Learners: Teaching Strategies that Work* by Larry Ferlazzo. Santa Barbara, CA: Linworth. Copyright © 2010.

Problem-Based Learning

In addition to the simple rubrics shared in this chapter, and the anonymous survey in Figure 4.7, teachers might want to consider two other tools in their assessment process.

One is being conscious of the levels of Bloom's taxonomy (<http://www.officeport.com/edu/blooms.htm>) and, depending upon the students' English level, consider explicitly teaching its structure. The higher the Bloom level that a student projects reach, the more effective the problem-based learning has been.

The second tool is using an evaluation form similar to the ones shared in previous chapters and different from the one in Figure 4.7. It could be as simple as asking, "What research questions do you think helped you learn the most and why?"

Here are sample responses to that question from one classroom:

✦ "I like all of them because they help me understand because it is about the world."

✦ "I like doing them because we used the imagination and we used our best abilities."

Free Voluntary Reading

One tool for evaluating this kind of reading is by including it in an anonymous survey asking how much students liked it and how much they learned from it. Another way to gauge its effectiveness is by having students complete two of the same clozes (fill-in-the-blanks) and read to the teacher from two passages three times during the year for one minute each. Teachers at Burbank High School and at other schools around the country that work with Pebble Creek Labs have found this to be a good barometer of reading progress. The clozes demonstrate vocabulary and comprehension, while the one-minute readings show reading fluency and decoding ability. Educators can easily develop clozes that have approximately 7–10 blanks for students to complete and identify reading passages appropriate for their class level. A cloze example (note that parts of it are written in a spirit of fun) is shown in Figure 4.8.

Luther Burbank High School has over 2,000 students and is in Sacramento, California. It is the best _____ in the whole world. It has great _____. My favorite teacher is Mr./Ms. _____. The school is so wonderful that _____ would pay to go there.

Students can learn world history, English, science, and _____ at the school. They can also have a lot of fun. Many _____ and Hmong students play soccer there. About 1/3 of the students are African American, 1/3 are Asian, and 1/3 are Latino. There are also some students from the Marshall Islands.

Many of the students are very good. Lorenzo, Chou, and Chia are some of the very best. Not all the students are good, though. Susan and Mai are very, very bad _____. Juan and _____ are also bad. They sometimes drive Mr. Ferlazzo crazy in _____ class. But they feel bad about it and have decided to bring a big plate of papaya salad every Friday as a way to tell him that they are sorry.

Every student in the world should be able to attend a school like Luther Burbank High School.

Figure 4.8 Cloze assessment example.

What Are the Challenges to Making Learning by Doing a Priority in the Classroom?

Most of the challenges covered in the previous stages of the organizing cycle fit with the idea of learning by doing, too. It's worth going back to those pages and reviewing them again. There are, however, two challenges that are particularly worth highlighting in this chapter.

The Textbook

Readers might be asking themselves, "How am I going to fit the inductive method and problem-based learning into using the required textbook?"

This is certainly a valid question if your school administrator and/or school district has a rule, and enforces it, that teachers must use a specific textbook the majority of the time. Fortunately, much of the material found in textbooks can also be reformulated into a data set or some kind of problem-based learning effort (an old community organizing saying goes "All organizing is reorganizing"). In addition to students gaining an understanding of the content, it might be surprising to see what other categories and questions students can develop and what teachable moments arise out of them. Use of the inductive method and problem-based learning does not have to occur all the time—consider experimenting with them periodically as a change of pace.

Student Accountability

Sometimes there is a concern that free voluntary reading does not have an appropriate level of student accountability. While the in-class reading is occurring, however, the educator is not a potted plant. She is circulating constantly and interacting with students around what they're reading. If a student does not appear to be seriously reading, the educator then helps the student identify a book he might be interested in through conversations about his interests—there is no great reward in not liking a book you are supposed to be reading for pleasure.

If students are also asked to read at home, an educator conversation with parents can be useful. Some educators require a reading log that students sign each night they have read, and some require that parents sign it, too.

When learning by doing is practiced in combination with other elements of the organizing cycle—particularly reflection, covered in the next chapter—it can be a powerful learning experience for educators and students alike.

CHAPTER 5

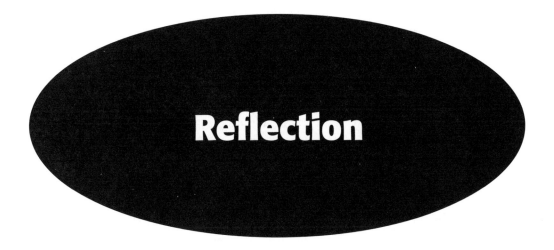

"In the past, I've asked you to pick examples of what you think was your best week in the quarter and explain why you think it was your best," I said to my class "You're going to do the same this quarter. But, in addition, I want you to complete these sentences."

I then passed out a sheet of paper that said:

_____ was my best moment in class because _____
_____. I helped make it my best moment by _____.
_____ was my worst moment in class because _____
_____. I could have made it better by _____.

I shared that this exercise has helped me to think back on times when I've done well and not so well, and to consider what I did to make it so good or not so good. I explained that I used this method to become a better teacher, and shared what I wrote on an overhead transparency:

> Watching students make their presentations to the other class was my best moment in class because I saw how hard everybody tried to do their best. I helped make it my best moment by having people work in small groups and by making sure they had time to practice.
> The lesson on topic sentences was my worst moment in class because I talked too much and it was not very interesting. I could have made it better by preparing a small group activity.

After checking for understanding—thumbs up, thumbs down, or thumbs in the middle—I then explained that after they filled out the sheet, they would make two posters. One would be for the best moment, and one for the worst. They would draw a picture for each and copy down what they wrote at the bottom of their picture. As a model, I showed students my artistically challenged poster.

After students were finished, they shared their creations in small groups, including the following:

Best

Ma: "Presentation was my best moment in class because I want to shows my word to other people I see. I helped make it a great moment by read louder and clearly" (Ma's poster is shown in Figure 5.1).

Pade: "Working in partners was my best moment in class because when we read together you can help each other. I helped make it a great moment by helping my partner."

Tou Yang: "Go to computer lab was the best moment because at this time we have a lot of fun with computer. I helped make it a great moment by help other students."

Worst

Yong: "Singing was my worst moment in class because I don't like to sing. I could have made it better by trying."

Tou Yang: "The final project was my worst moment in class because I lose some of my work. I could have made it better by keeping all my work."

Afterwards, Jose came up to me and said, "I like this class a lot, but you make us think too much!"

Students, with modeling and scaffolding, were asked to push themselves to think differently and more deeply about their work in class. They considered not just what they did well or not so well but what they had done to make those results happen. They then shared their reflections with their classmates so that others could learn from their thinking. In addition to practicing their English reading, writing, listening, and speaking skills, they helped make sure they avoided what T. S. Eliot described: "We had the experience but missed the meaning."

What Do You Mean by Reflection?

The word "reflection" comes from the Latin *reflexionem*—"a bending back." It is about bending back to think about what you're doing and what you've done, and to evaluate those thoughts and actions. Most importantly, it's about then taking those conclusions and applying them to future thinking and action.

Organizers often talk about all of us being sometimes composed of undigested or unprocessed actions. Without spending time on reflection, we might very well gain information, which is defined as "a collection of facts and data," but are less likely to come away with "knowledge," which is defined as "the confident understanding of a subject with the ability to use it for a specific purpose" (<http://en.wikipedia.org/wiki/Knowledge>).

Organizers often cite the work of philosopher Hannah Arendt when they talk about the importance of reflection. Arendt wrote a book after she observed the trial of Adolf Eichmann, the architect of the Holocaust. She shared that she had expected to see a monster. Instead, she was shocked to see a man who was mechanical, bureaucratic, and thoughtless. She began thinking that evil was more the result of the absence of thinking and reflection, which she described in a famous phrase as the "banality of evil" (Arendt 252).

Though Eichmann is obviously an extreme case, this point is also important for those of us who are not perpetrating evil. If we don't think and reflect, we can be mechanical and live our

Figure 5.1 "My Best Moment" student example.

lives by a formula. We can fail to calculate the consequences of what we do, and we can make the same mistakes over and over again that can lead to personal and, sometimes, social destructiveness. We can learn the *facts* but miss the opportunity to develop an *understanding*.

Another contrast that organizers often make is that reflection is critical in order to develop *judgment*, while the lack of it leads to only *opinion*. According to Dictionary.com, "judgment" means "the ability to make a decision, or form an opinion objectively, authoritatively, and wisely, especially in matters affecting action." Dictionary.com says an "opinion" is "a personal view, attitude, or appraisal."

Organizers emphasize the distinction even further by believing that it's important to include social interaction in the reflective process so that people can gain the maturity of having an open mind, a belief shared by education theorist John Dewey (Rodgers 856, 861).

John Dewey repeatedly stressed the important role reflection plays in learning. Professor Carol Rodgers summarized Dewey's perspective:

> The function of reflection is to make meaning: to formulate the "relationships and continuities" among the elements of an experience, between that experience and other experiences, between that experience and the knowledge that one carries, and between that knowledge and the knowledge produced by thinkers other than oneself. (848)

The recognition of reflection as a critical component of learning, of course, goes even further back than Dewey. Socrates "advocated reflection . . . to know better something which in some sense we know already; to know it better in the sense of coming to know it in a different and better way" (Waxman, Freiberg, Vaughn, and Weil 11).

What Does Research Say about Using Reflection in the Classroom?

Extensive research has been done on the value of student reflection. This section will divide those findings into three parts: findings from general education research, from brain-based learning, and from analyses of student self-assessment.

Education Research

Robert J. Marzano, the well-known and respected education researcher, has recognized the importance of student reflection in the learning process. He calls it "the final step in a comprehensive approach to actively processing information" (Marzano 57). He suggests that educators ask students to respond to one of three reflective prompts:

✦ What they were right about and wrong about.

✦ How confident they are about what they have learned.

✦ What they did well during the experience and what they could have done better. (Marzano 57)

A survey of several studies on critical reflection found that it is a challenge to encourage students to engage in reflective activities. However, the authors, Neville Hatton and David Smith, suggest that one key variable—talking with others—is "a powerful strategy for fostering reflective action . . . It can provide a safe environment within which self-revelation can take place."

Ongoing written journals are one of the tools often used for reflective activity. A study by Maria Dantas-Whitney, though, of an English language learner class had students use an audio journal. The results showed that the journals were valuable for speaking practice and self-evaluation.

Tech Tips—Audio Journals

Snapvine (<http://www.snapvine.com/home>) lets students easily e-mail voice messages they record. They can also save them to their own free account. It's a voice journal that they can let others access, and those others can in turn comment on what was said in the journal.

Brain-Based Learning

Experts on brain-based learning have also described how reflection is a critical element in the learning process. Without it, "teachers may expend a great deal of effort in orchestrating an experience, only to discover that students have absorbed very little (Caine and Caine 156). Brain researchers like the Caines use the same terminology that Marzano used—reflection is necessary for "active processing." The Caines go on to say that reflection "is the path to understanding, rather than simply to memory" (156) and offer their own set of questions for students to ask themselves:

✦ What did I do?

✦ Why did I do it?

✦ What did I learn? (157)

Neurologist and teacher Judy Willis agrees, and points out that another reason this kind of metacognition (thinking about one's thinking) is important is because it "shows [students] a tool they will use again. It could ultimately become one of the distinct learning behaviors that enhances their competence and confidence and helps them become optimal learners . . . Because . . . students were asked open-ended questions about what they found interesting, what they were reminded of, and what they still want to know about, they will be able to take the lesson beyond the classroom door, perhaps even into the lunchroom in a discussion with a classmate, or to the family dinner table" (Willis 33).

Student Self-Assessment

Student self-evaluation, also known as student self-assessment, is considered by many researchers to be an element of student reflection because of its reinforcement of metacognition (Srimavin and Darasawang 1). Carol Rholheiser and John Ross write that studies have shown that self-evaluation, "defined as students judging the quality of their work, based on evidence and explicit criteria, for the purpose of doing better work in the future," can be a "powerful technique because of its impact on student performance through enhanced self-efficacy and increased intrinsic motivation." Rholheiser and Ross go on to emphasize the importance of using an extensively scaffolded approach to ensure the success of such an effort.

Research in Action—Learning Topic Sentences and Supporting Details

The intermediate English class was learning how to write a persuasive essay. After an introductory lesson on developing topic sentences and following them with supporting details, the teacher reviewed several good model paragraphs on the overhead with the entire class highlighting why they were well written. Next, the teacher shared paragraphs of lower quality, which the entire class discussed and graded. Next, students received copies of several additional paragraphs of mixed quality. They were divided into pairs and graded each one and explained their reasons. A class discussion and review followed. Student final essays that year not only included much better topic sentences and supporting details than in previous years, but all students gave themselves the same grade for that element of the essay that the teacher would have given them.

What Are Examples of Using Reflection in the Classroom?

There are a number of ways to help students focus on reflection in class, including just periodically asking students at the end of a class to respond to some of the questions suggested by Marzano and the Caines. You might, however, want to be a bit more strategic in order to make it a more central part of your students' learning. Some specific ideas follow.

A Learning Log or Reflection Journal

"Learning log" and "reflection journal" are two names that have been used to describe a collection of regularly written comments by students (an electronic version of these will be discussed later in the chapter). It's probably easier for students to have them in a binder, so the entries can be collected one at a time after each is written, and then returned later. At perhaps their least useful (at least for the purpose of reflection), they are sometimes used as a place for students to take notes during class. Others, like teacher author Rick Wormeli, suggest they be used for student summarizations of lessons (106). They can also primarily be used for students' reflections, or for a combination of the three purposes.

Here are some potential questions to ask students to respond to in their journals in addition to the ones shared in the research section of this chapter:

✦ What is the most important thing you learned today and why do you think it's important?

✦ What could you have done differently today to learn more, or to help others learn more?

✦ What are two things you could tell your parents that you learned in class today, and why would you choose those two things?

✦ What are two questions related to this lesson that you would still like to know the answer to? Why do you want to find those answers?

✦ What was the hardest thing you did in class today? Why was it so hard?

✦ What was the easiest thing you did in class today? Why was it so easy?

✦ How can you use what you learned today in your life outside of school?

◆ What's one thing you feel you did well this week and why do you think you did it so well?

◆ What are your ideas about how we could have improved the class today (this week, this year)?

◆ What was the most helpful (and least helpful) thing we did today to help you learn English? What did it help or not help?

◆ Do you understand vowels (or a subject that was studied that day) a little more today than you did yesterday? If you do, why?

◆ What are the three class activities you liked the best this semester, and why did you like them?

◆ What are the three class activities you liked the least this semester, and why didn't you like them?

◆ What did you learn today that you can teach your little brother, sister, or cousin? How would you teach it?

◆ If you were the teacher, how would you have taught today's lesson and why would you have done it that way?

Less proficient English language learners can be provided sentence starters to use to respond to the questions or even draw pictures instead. For example, for the last question listed, students could be given this structure: "I learned _____. I would teach him/her by first _____. Then I would _____."
Here is Yong's answer using this sentence starter:

> I learned how to practice new words and vowels. I would teach him by first showing them to sing a song and then I would teach them about the homework with the sounds.

Yang Mee wrote:

> I learned how to sound out letter "A" I would teach him by first telling them to try to sound out letter "an" and then show them how to write letter "a."

The questions certainly do not have to be limited to what is happening in your class or even in school. Getting an idea of how students are experiencing their other classes can be useful knowledge for both you and their other teachers if you choose to share it, and learning what challenges they might be facing at home or their dreams for the future are obviously helpful, too. In addition, the habit of reflecting about all parts of their lives is a discipline needed by lifelong learners, so it is important to give students the opportunity to develop this habit. These types of questions could include:

◆ How are things going at home for you right now? What's good and not so good, and how are they making you feel and why?

◆ What classes are going well for you? Why do you think they are going so well? What classes are not going so well for you? Why do you think they are not going well?

◆ What is one thing you want to do better this semester and why?

◆ What is one thing you've done that you feel proud of? Why do you feel proud of it?

◆ What job would you like to get after you're finished with school? Why do you want that job?

◆ Describe your life 10 years from now? Why are the things you've described important to you?

Having students share what they wrote with a partner or a few other students, and then giving them the opportunity to revise their reflections, serves two purposes—it enhances student relationships, and it helps students move from opinion to judgment.

The student projects in this section correlate with California English language development (ELD) domains 1, 5, and 6.

Classroom Story—Students Writing Honestly

It's important to emphasize that students should write their reflections honestly and that they won't be penalized if they write something that respectfully critiques the class or the teacher. One day I asked students to respond to this question:

"How is this class different, and how is it the same, as other classes they were taking?"

Most students wrote that they did a lot more reading and writing in this class, and that they had a lot more fun, too. One student responded:

"This class is the greatest. Mr. Ferlazzo is the coolest teacher. We get to do fun stuff. I love this class!"

Then, in parentheses, right below it he added:

"Please, please, Mr. Ferlazzo, give me an A."

Another time I asked students to consider what they had learned during the past week. One student wrote: "I didn't learn anything, but that was okay because Mr. Ferlazzo tried his best."

Metaphors and Similes for Reflection

Having students create metaphors or similes comparing how they were at the beginning of the semester and how they are at the end, and then where they want to be at the end of the year, is another potential lesson idea that could be modified in any number of ways.

Metaphor or Simile Student Reflection Lesson Plan

Instructional Objectives

Students will:

1. Develop an understanding of the concepts of metaphors and similes.

2. Apply their understanding of metaphor and simile toward reflection on their life experiences.

3. Write a grammatically correct sentence using a metaphor or simile.

4. Practice English oral skills in sharing their sentences with other classmates.

Duration

Two 55-minute class periods.

English Language Development Standards California English Language Development (ELD) Domains

1. Students use English for everyday communication in socially and culturally appropriate ways and apply listening and speaking skills and strategies in the classroom.

5. Students will write well-organized, clear, and coherent text in a variety of academic genres.

6. Students will apply the conventions of standard English usage orally and in writing.

Materials

1. Poster paper and color markers.

2. Transparency simile sentence starters.

3. Model poster.

Procedure

First Day

1. Teacher says, "I am going to ask you a question. After I ask it, don't say anything until I say to speak. For now, just think about the answer. My question is: When you see someone you love, does it make you feel hot, cold, or nothing at all? Think about it for a few seconds. Now I want you to share your answer with a neighbor. How many said hot? How many said cold? How many said nothing?" (Most will say hot.)

2. Teacher then asks the class if the sun makes them feel hot, cold, or nothing. After students respond, the teacher writes on front board: "Love is like the sun, because they both make you feel hot." Teacher explains that this is called a simile—it is saying one thing is like another thing. Teacher checks for understanding—thumbs up, thumbs down, or thumbs in the middle.

3. Teacher asks, "What does a brain do?" using the think, pair, and share method again. He writes answers on the board, and then asks, "What does a computer do?" After writing the answers to that question on the board, too, he writes out a simile using some of the words, such as "A brain is a like a computer because they both think."

4. Teacher then puts a transparency on the overhead projector, only showing the first sentence. It reads: "This class is like a _____ because _____." He instructs the class to work silently and complete the sentence. After a few minutes, students can share with a partner and then with the entire class. Teacher writes some on the sheet.

5. The teacher then shows other sentences for students to complete: "School cafeteria food is like _____ because _____." "Home is like _____ because _____." "Love is like _____ because _____."

6. Teacher explains that when you use the word "like" it is called a simile. When you don't have the word "like" in it, it's called a metaphor. The teacher then converts several of the similes that the class has reviewed into metaphors.

7. Teacher explains that students will make a poster showing two similes or metaphors (they can choose which one they want to use). One will show the kind of person they were at the

beginning of the year and the other will show who they are now. Teacher shows a model (explaining that no one can use the simile he has used) he has made: at the beginning of the year she was an ABC book, and now she's a English newspaper ("I was an ABC book before because I didn't know any English, but now I'm a newspaper because I can read and speak English much better"). Or, the teacher could use a growing plant, a bike and a race car, and so forth. The teacher just should not model more than one example.

8. Students are given the rest of the class period to start their posters. They are told they will have 30 minutes the next day to finish it. Teacher circulates to ensure students understand the assignment.

Second Day

1. The first 30 minutes are spent working on their poster.

2. Then students will share them in small groups.

3. Teacher summarizes that the point of the lesson was for them not only to learn about metaphors and similes but also to see the importance of stepping back sometimes to think about their lives and how much progress they have made.

Assessment

1. Students can be asked to grade themselves on if they completed an accurate sentence using a metaphor or simile, and if they tried their best to illustrate it. If they did, they should give themselves an "A." If they did not, they should give themselves the grade they think they deserve. Teacher can then review the assessments.

Extensions

1. Students can use Web tools to create online multimedia versions of their metaphors/similes.

Students could also share what they were one year earlier and compare themselves to what they are now. They don't necessarily even need to draw themselves as metaphors if that is too complex of a concept. Xeng drew himself as a bike at the beginning of the year, and then as a racing car. He wrote "I was a bike before, but now I'm a car because I work hard, study hard, and read more." Pao Choua drew himself as a slow turtle at the beginning of a race in September, but in June he was a fast rabbit who had won "because now I'm a smart student and studied hard."

Other Special Reflection Projects

Expanded reflective projects could also be done as a change of pace and to reach out to other learning styles. Drawing a comic strip, performing a short skit with others, or showing a video are all other ways students can show their reflections in response to a particular question.

Another idea is suggested by Rick Wormeli, who writes about a 3-2-1 activity:

> ask your students to write the numerals 3, 2, and 1 down the left side of the their paper, leaving a few lines of space between each number. Then post or announce prompts for each number, asking students to write three of something, two of something, and then one of something. For example, students might explain three new things they learned from the lesson, two areas in which they are still confused, and one way they might apply what they've learned to another area . . . [it] can also be expressed artistically or orally. (Wormeli 39)

The student projects in this section correlate with California ELD domains 1, 5, and 6.

Reading and Watching about Reflection

Another way to emphasize the importance of reflection is to identify stories that show the impact on a person of taking time to reflect or *not* taking the time to reflect. This could range from reviewing a very short excerpt from Franz Kafka's "The Metamorphosis," showing the main character Gregor turning into a cockroach partially because of his mindless day-to-day mechanical life (believe it or not, there is an online video game about Kafka's life that students could play in conjunction with such a read-aloud—it's called Kafkamesto: <http://www.abc.net.au/gameon/kafkamesto/>), to a children's folktale. Another book to consider is Menchin's *Taking a Bath with the Dog and Other Things That Make Me Happy* about a little girl exploring happiness.

School librarians might be particularly helpful in identifying reading material appropriate for a class. Clozes, read-alouds, and using reading strategies are just a few of the language-development strategies that could be used with these passages in addition to helping students learn the importance of reflection.

Video clips from movies showing the same message could be shown using the English language learner instructional method called "Back to the Screens," described by Laurel Pollard in her book, *Zero Prep For Beginners.*. In a modified version, the educator divides the class into pairs, with one group facing the TV and the other with their backs to it. Then, after turning off the sound, the educator begins playing the movie. The person who can see the screen tells the other person what is happening. Then, after awhile, the groups switch around. Afterwards, the pairs write a chronological sequence of what happened, which is shared in class. Finally, everyone watches the clip, with sound, together.

The student projects in this section correlate with California ELD domains 1, 2, 3, 4, and 6.

How Can Technology Be Used to Reinforce Reflection?

Technology offers several value-added opportunities to promote student reflection, in addition to providing a periodic change of pace.

Online Journals

Students using blogs for learning logs or reflection journals offer a number of advantages over using paper ones. For the student, automatic online checkers for grammar and spelling are another learning opportunity; it makes it easier to revise their writing; free text-to-speech Web tools like Odiogo (<http://www.odiogo.com/>) can let students hear what they write and help with pronunciation and composition; and other students can easily write comments on each other's reflections. For the educator, it is easier logistically to read journals online instead of having to deal with the bulk of paper; plus, they are clearer to read. Each student can have his or her own blog, or there can be one class blog where the teacher posts the reflection question and all students respond in the same place. See Appendix 1 for more details on blogs.

Word Clouds

Wordle (<http://www.wordle.net/>) and Tag Crowd (<http://tagcrowd.com/>) are two free Web applications that let users upload a file or Web site, and then return a word cloud—a graphic representation showing the frequency of word use. In other words, the more often the word is used, the larger the word would appear in the word cloud. Users can also determine the shape of the cloud.

Having students regularly use these tools with their blogs, or with particular papers they write, is an excellent way for them to reflect on why certain words were used so often and others so seldom. For example, if the word "angry" shows up in a large size, that could prompt a students to consider the source of his anger and write about it. Everyone's blog posts could also be uploaded to see what a class-wide word cloud would show.

Multimedia and Other Artistic Projects

Just as in the classroom, a video, slideshow, or comic representation of student reflections can be posted online. Besides providing opportunities for peers to leave comments on them, this method also lets students develop computer skills. Students can use cell phones video recorders or inexpensive camcorders.

Free sites that students can use for multimedia creation include Glogster (<http://www.glogster. com/edu/>) and WallWisher (<http://www.wallwisher.com/wall/>), both of which are very easy tools for students to use to share their reflections in creative-looking text, videos, and photos (either their own or ones they grab off the Web), and with drawings. There are also sites where students can even sing their reflections and record them online. In addition, English language learners can make simple animations that demonstrate their reflections fairly easily at DoInk (<http://www.doink.com/>). DoInk has a strict and proactive policy to ensure classroom-appropriate content on the site. More details can be found in Appendix 1.

The student projects in this section correlate with California ELD domains 1, 2, 5, and 6.

How Do You Assess Reflection?

Research cited earlier in this chapter clearly demonstrates that providing structured opportunities for student reflection can enhance learning and academic achievement. If educators are not clear on the value of reflection, they can also do their own research project by making reflection a key element of one class and having another one as a control group where it is less of a central tool. Teachers can learn more about how to structure such research by reading *The Reflective Educator's Guide to Classroom Research,* by Nancy Fichtman Dana and Diane Yendol-Hoppey. In fact, similar research efforts could be done to assess any element in the organizing cycle.

Another way to assess reflection's effectiveness is to ask the students themselves. Here are three questions, and examples of real answers written by students, that teachers can ask students at the end of a semester or year using an anonymous survey such as the one shown in Figure 5.2.

1. When you're not in this classroom, do you spend much time thinking about what we have learned in class? Why or why not?
   ✦ Yes, because it help me learned how to speak English. This class is important to me because this class help know how to speak English.

◆ Yes, sometime I don't understand somethings. I spend my time to discuss with my friends.

◆ I think about what I have learned in class because sometimes we're learning things which I'm worried about or I'm interesting in them.

2. What things that you learned in class this year do you think you'll most remember? Why?

◆ I think learning about citizenship help me most to remember because I have to use to become a citizen.

◆ The more people you have the more power you have. Because I think going to use in the future.

3. Does having to answer these kinds of questions, and the questions you answered when we kept learning logs, help you learn? Why or why not?

◆ Yes it help me learn because when you do the Learning Logs after you read you have to think what you learn.

◆ I learned so much doing this because I review that things that I read or hear.

◆ I think answering these kinds of questions help me learn because make me think about it.

◆ I think these kid of questions help me learn because they make me overthink what we've been doing and learning.

◆ Yes, because I can share my own opinions to other people as students in class.

◆ Yes, because they help me understand how to answer a question.

◆ Yes, because it helps me write sentence and learn English.

◆ Yes, the questions that you can ask in class help me to know how to say thing important to my life.

STUDENT REFLECTION SURVEY

1. When you're not in this classroom, do you spend much time thinking about what we have learned in class? Why or why not?

2. What things that you learned in class this year do you think you'll most remember? Why?

3. Does having to answer these kinds of questions, and the questions you answered when we kept learning logs, help you learn? Why or why not?

Figure 5.2   Student reflection survey.
From *English Language Learners: Teaching Strategies that Work* by Larry Ferlazzo. Santa Barbara, CA: Linworth. Copyright © 2010.

What Are the Challenges to Using Reflection in the Classroom?

Again, many of the challenges in previous chapters may very well apply here as well. One of the particular issues that might face students and teachers about reflection is getting to the "Why?"

Taking time to reflect may be outside of the experience of many students and, perhaps, of educators, as well. Many students might, at first, try to get by with writing answers that are not very deep. If they are asked "What are the three class activities you liked this semester and why did you like them?" they might respond to the first part of the question and ignore the second half.

One way to respond to this problem is by using the instructional method highlighted at the beginning of chapter 4—concept attainment. An educator can take several student responses that answer both parts of the question, and several that do not. Put them under "Yes" and "No" columns in the front of the room, and students will quickly see what the differences are. The point, however, is not necessarily to use student reflections for grammar or spelling correction—there will be plenty of other student writings for those examples. Correcting those elements may make students more reluctant to take risks in their reflection writing. Use concept attainment, instead, to help students begin to learn how to look within themselves.

Saul Alinsky said that "organizations need action as an individual needs oxygen." (Alinsky 120). It can also be said that a classroom needs learning by doing as an individual needs oxygen. But just as a person can be damaged by getting too much oxygen, the same might happen to students if they are constantly doing without taking time to reflect.

Tikal is a magnificent Mayan city in Guatemala. If you climb to the top of one of the pyramids, all you can see is the forest canopy and the tops of two or three more pyramids jutting above it. Leading good reflections are the same way—one needs to help students develop the capacity to move beyond the canopy composed of all the tasks they are involved with and to develop the judgment to see the truly important tops of pyramids.

Afterword

Years ago, a member of one our community groups was describing the contrast between two organizers she had worked with. She had learned a lot of information from one, she said, but she had learned how to think from the other.

Of course, it doesn't have to be an either/or situation. In fact, it's critical that good teachers do both.

We don't want to come to the classroom and *shove* stuff at and into students. Nor do we want to *sell* to them. Rather, an educator/organizer is one who risks helping students to *share* and to *seek*.

By keeping the elements of the organizing cycle in mind—building relationships, accessing prior knowledge through stories, developing student leadership, learning by doing, and reflection—we can use them not just as a guide for individual lessons but also for the flow of a unit plan, a school year, and, really, for an effective life.

APPENDIX 1

Technology Resources

This appendix will share details about technology resources discussed in each chapter. Some sites are mentioned in more than one chapter. If that's the case, instead of repeating the information, it will be located in the earliest chapter where it has been mentioned.

For additional information beyond these resources, you can visit these sites:

✦ Larry Ferlazzo's Websites of the Day (<http://larryferlazzo.edublogs.org/>) is a popular resource-sharing blog for teachers focused on using technology with English language learners. It includes over 400 regularly updated "The Best . . ." lists of resources ("The Best Sites For Beginning ELL's," "The Best Online Slideshow Tools," etc.).

✦ Larry Ferlazzo also has a Web site designed for student self-access that contains over 9,000 categorized links accessible to English language learners (<http://larryferlazzo.com/english.html>).

Chapter 1: Building Relationships

Online slideshow tools accessible to English language learners:

✦ Bookr (<http://www.pimpampum.net/bookr/>)

✦ Smile Slideshow (<http://www.colgate.com/ColgateSmile/mashup.srv>)

✦ PhotoPeach (<http://photopeach.com/>)

✦ VoiceThread (<http://voicethread.com>)—allows audio

✦ Show Beyond (<http://www.showbeyond.com/show/home>)—allows audio

- SlideSix (<http://slidesix.com/>)—allows audio
- "The Best Ways to Create Online Slideshows" (<http://larryferlazzo.edublogs.org/2008/05/06/the-best-ways-to-create-online-slideshows/>)

Student Timelines

- xTimeline (<http://www.xtimeline.com/index.aspx>)
- "The Best Tools for Making Online Timelines" (<http://larryferlazzo.edublogs.org/2008/08/06/the-best-tools-for-making-online-timelines/>)

Student Online Safety

Sites that provide good information for teachers to know about student safety and legal issues related to online student work:

- The Edublogger (<http://theedublogger.edublogs.org/2008/02/13/tips-on-blogging-with-students/>)
- "Internet Safety for Teachers and Students" (<http://www.k12science.org/internetsafety.html>)
- "The Best Teacher Resources for Online Student Safety and Legal Issues" (<http://larryferlazzo.edublogs.org/2009/08/10/the-best-teacher-resources-for-online-student-safety-legal-issues/>)

Sites Where English Language Learners Can Learn about Online Safety

- Cyber Café (<http://www.thinkuknow.co.uk/(X(1)S(1fzvor455xt335vof51qr0b3))/8_10/cybercafe/cafe/base.aspx?AspxAutoDetectCookieSupport=1>)
- "The Best Sites for Learning Online Safety" (<http://larryferlazzo.edublogs.org/2009/08/02/the-best-sites-for-learning-online-safety/>)

Copyright

Sites that provide helpful information on how students can legally use other people's images, videos, and music in student projects:

- "Fair Use, Copyright, Plagiarism . . . What Does It All Mean?" (<http://www.vrml.k12.la.us/curriculum/fairuse/fairuse.htm>)
- "The Best Resources to Learn about Copyright Issues" (<http://larryferlazzo.edublogs.org/2009/08/10/the-best-resources-to-learn-about-copyright-issues/>)

Blogs

Sites that provide free blogs (online journals) and offer comment moderation. In other words, a comment on someone's online work has to be approved before it is published. Two, especially the first one listed, are used by many teachers:

✦ Edublogs (<http://edublogs.org/>)

✦ Posterous (<http://posterous.com/>)

✦ "The Best Places Where Students Can Write Online" (<http://larryferlazzo.edublogs.org/2008/10/19/the-best-places-where-students-can-write-online/>)

✦ "The Best Sources of Advice on Student Blogging" (<http://larryferlazzo.edublogs.org/2008/12/26/the-best-sources-for-advice-on-student-blogging/>)

Reading

✦ Starfall (<http://www.starfall.com/>)—beginning

✦ Literactive (<http://www.literactive.com/Home/index.asp>)—beginning

✦ Speekaboos (<http://www.speakaboos.com/>)—beginning

✦ Awesome Stories (<http://www.awesomestories.com/>)—intermediate

✦ "The Best Websites to Help Beginning Readers" (<http://larryferlazzo.edublogs.org/2008/01/22/the-best-websites-to-help-beginning-readers/>)

✦ "The Best Websites for Beginning Older Readers" (<http://larryferlazzo.edublogs.org/2008/01/23/the-best-websites-for-beginning-older-readers/>)

✦ "The Best Websites for Intermediate Readers" (<http://larryferlazzo.edublogs.org/2008/01/26/the-best-websites-for-intermediate-readers/>)

Online Language Learning Games and Activities

✦ Henny Jellema's Online Total Physical Response Exercises (<http://www.digischool.nl/oefenen/hennyjellema/engels/tpr/voorbladtpr.htm>)

✦ USA Learns (<http://usalearns.org/>)

✦ "The Best Sites for K-12 Beginning English Language Learners" (<http://larryferlazzo.edublogs.org/2009/01/16/the-best-sites-for-k-12-beginning-english-language-learners/>)

✦ "The Best Sites for K-12 Intermediate English Language Learners" (<http://larryferlazzo.edublogs.org/2009/03/14/the-best-sites-for-k-12-intermediate-english-language-learners/>)

Viral Marketing

✦ "Samuel L. Jackson, My ESL Students, and Me" (<http://www.techlearning.com/article/7144>)

✦ "The Best Ways to Create Online Content Easily and Quickly" (<http://larryferlazzo.edublogs.org/2009/07/18/the-best-ways-to-create-online-content-easily-quickly-%E2%80%94-2009/>)

Online Video Games

✦ "Free Online Games Develop ESL Students' Language Skills" (<http://www.techlearning.com/article/8270>)

✦ "The Best Websites for Creating Online Learning Games" (<http://larryferlazzo.edublogs.org/2008/04/21/the-best-websites-for-creating-online-learning-games/>)

Chapter 2: Accessing Prior Knowledge through Stories
Creating Online Maps

✦ MapTrot (<http://maptrot.com/>)

✦ MapBuzz (<http://www.mapbuzz.com/>)

✦ "The Best Map-Making Sites on the Web" (<http://larryferlazzo.edublogs.org/2008/12/03/the-best-map-making-sites-on-the-web/>)

Annotating Webpages

✦ Blerp (<http://www.blerp.com/browser/index>)

✦ RhooIt (<http://roohit.com/site/home.php>)

✦ "Best Applications for Annotating Websites" (<http://larryferlazzo.edublogs.org/2008/12/18/best-applications-for-annotating-websites/>)

Digital Storytelling

✦ Make Beliefs Comix (<http://www.makebeliefscomix.com/Comix/>)

✦ Dvolver Moviemaker (<http://www.dfilm.com/live/moviemaker.html>)

✦ Bombay TV (<http://www.grapheine.com/bombaytv/index.php?lang=uk>)

✦ File2.ws (<http://file2.ws/>)

✦ "The Best Digital Storytelling Resources" (<http://larryferlazzo.edublogs.org/2009/04/15/the-best-digital-storytelling-resources/>)

✦ "The Best Ways to Make Comic Strips Online" (<http://larryferlazzo.edublogs.org/2008/06/04/the-best-ways-to-make-comic-strips-online/>)

✦ "The Best Ways for Students to Create Online Animations" (<http://larryferlazzo.edublogs.org/2008/05/11/the-best-ways-for-students-to-create-online-animations/>)

✦ "The Best Ways for Students to Create Online Videos (Using Someone Else's Content)" (<http://larryferlazzo.edublogs.org/2008/05/14/the-best-ways-for-students-to-create-online-videos-using-someone-else%E2%80%99s-content/>)

* "The Best Sources for Advice on Using Flip Video Cameras" (<http://larryferlazzo.edublogs.org/2009/06/05/the-best-sources-for-advice-on-using-flip-video-cameras/>)

Text-To-Speech and Pronunciation

* YAKiToMe (<http://yakitome.com/>)
* Read the Words (<http://readthewords.com/>)
* Vocaroo (<http://vocaroo.com/>)
* Screentoaster (<http://www.screentoaster.com/record>)
* Daft Doggy (<http://www.daftdoggy.com/recorder/record.php>)
* "The Best Websites for Practicing English Pronunciation" (<http://larryferlazzo.edublogs.org/2008/03/31/the-best-websites-for-learning-english-pronunciation/>)

Finding Sister Classes

* "The Best Ways to Find Other Classes for Joint Online Projects" (<http://larryferlazzo.edublogs.org/2009/05/30/the-best-ways-to-find-other-classes-for-joint-online-projects/>)

Developing Personal Learning Networks

* "The Best Ways ESL/EFL/ELL Teachers Can Develop Personal Learning Networks" (http://larryferlazzo.edublogs.org/2009/11/07/the-best-ways-esleflell-teachers-can-develop-personal-learning-networks/>)

Chapter 3: Identifying and Mentoring Students' Leadership Potential
Virtual Field Trips

* "The Best Resources for Finding and Creating Virtual Field Trips" (<http://larryferlazzo.edublogs.org/2009/08/11/the-best-resources-for-finding-and-creating-virtual-field-trips/>)

Speaking and Listening

* "The Best Listening Sites for English Language Learners" (<http://larryferlazzo.edublogs.org/2008/05/28/the-best-listening-sites-for-english-language-learners/>)
* "The Best Sites to Practice Speaking English" (<http://larryferlazzo.edublogs.org/2008/03/17/the-best-sites-to-practice-speaking-english/>)
* "The Best Websites for Developing English Conversational Skills" (<http://larryferlazzo.edublogs.org/2008/04/05/the-best-sites-for-developing-english-conversational-skills/>)

How-to Sites

✦ Graspr (<http://www.graspr.com/>)

✦ Monkey See (<http://www.monkeysee.com/>)

✦ "The Best Online Instructional Video Sites" (<http://larryferlazzo.edublogs.org/2008/07/24/the-best-online-instructional-video-sites/>)

Chapter 4: Learning by Doing
Picture Data Sets

✦ Middlespot (<http://middlespot.com/search.php>)

✦ Wallwisher (<http://www.wallwisher.com/>)

✦ "The Best Social Bookmarking Applications for English Language Learners and Other Students" (<http://larryferlazzo.edublogs.org/2008/04/16/the-best-social-bookmarking-applications-for-english-language-learners-other-students/>)

Neighborhood Analyses

✦ ZipSkinny (<http://zipskinny.com/>)

✦ Walk Score (<http://www.walkscore.com/>)

✦ Housing Mapper (<http://www.housingmaps.com/>)

✦ "Student Neighborhood Maps" (<http://larryferlazzo.com/Student%20Work.html#neighborhood>)

Online Printable Books

✦ Reading A-Z (<http://www.readinga-z.com/>)

✦ "The Best Sources for Free and Accessible Printable Books" (<http://larryferlazzo.edublogs.org/2009/07/31/the-best-sources-for-free-accessible-printable-books/>)

Webquests and Internet Scavenger Hunts

✦ Quest Garden (<http://questgarden.com/>)

✦ Zunal (<http://www.zunal.com/>)

✦ Teachers First (<http://www.teachersfirst.com/summer/webquest/quest-b.shtml>)

✦ "The Best Places to Find (and Create) Internet Scavenger Hunts and Webquests" (<http://larryferlazzo.edublogs.org/2009/02/15/the-best-sources-for-internet-scavenger-hunts-webquests/>)

Writing for an Authentic Audience

- ✦ Timelines (<http://timelines.com/>)
- ✦ Knol (<http://knol.google.com/k/?hd=ns>)
- ✦ Ruba (<http://www.ruba.com/>)
- ✦ Next Step (<http://www.nextstop.com/>)
- ✦ Project Label (<https://projectlabel.org/index.php>)
- ✦ Lists of Bests (<http://www.listsofbests.com/>)
- ✦ The Top Tens (<http://www.the-top-tens.com/>)
- ✦ Tar Heel Reader (<http://tarheelreader.org/>)
- ✦ Tikatok (<http://www.tikatok.com/>)
- ✦ "The Best Places Where Students Can Write for an 'Authentic Audience'" (<http://larry ferlazzo.edublogs.org/2009/04/01/the-best-places-where-students-can-write-for-an-authentic-audience/>)
- ✦ "The Best Places Where Students Can Create Online Learning/Teaching Objects for an 'Authentic Audience'" (<http://larryferlazzo.edublogs.org/2009/04/04/the-best-places-where-students-can-create-online-learningteaching-objects-for-an-authentic-audience/>)

Chapter 5: Reflection
Audio Journals

- ✦ Snapvine (<http://www.snapvine.com/home>)

Word Clouds

- ✦ Wordle (<http://www.wordle.net/>)
- ✦ Tag Crowd (<http://tagcrowd.com/>)

Multimedia Projects

- ✦ Glogster (<http://www.glogster.com/edu/>)
- ✦ WallWisher (<http://www.wallwisher.com/wall/>),
- ✦ DoInk (<http://www.doink.com/>)
- ✦ "The Best Art Websites for Learning English" (<http://larryferlazzo.edublogs.org/2008/02/01/the-best-art-websites-for-learning-english/>)
- ✦ "The Best Online Sites for Creating Music" (<http://larryferlazzo.edublogs.org/2008/10/01/the-best-online-sites-for-creating-music/>)

APPENDIX 2

Classroom Games

"Trick them into thinking they aren't learning and they do," says Roland "Prez" Pryzbylewski, a teacher in the HBO television series "The Wire." In the show, he gets a very challenging group of kids to learn math by showing them how to determine odds as they play dice for Monopoly money.

Learning another language can be a challenging and often frustrating experience for many of our students. No matter how motivated students are, a good teacher must have many instructional tools at his/her disposal to help students *engage* in the class and not have to *endure* it. Games are one of those.

Judy Willis, neurologist and teacher, writes that students, especially adolescents, are more likely to store information as part of their long-term memory and make them available for later retrieval through participating in activities they enjoy (20). Researcher Robert. J. Marzano also endorses learning games as an "engagement activity" that can result in increased student academic achievement (103).

Here are six criteria to consider for any game played in the classroom:

1. It requires little or no preparation on the teacher's part.
2. Any needed materials are developed by the students themselves—the preparation for the games in itself is a language learning experience.

A version of this appendix originally appeared in *Language Magazine*, and is reprinted with permission.

3. In addition to not costing teachers much time, they can also be done without costing any money.

4. The game is designed in a way to strongly encourage all students in the class to be engaged at all times.

5. The game, after being modeled by the teacher a number of times, can periodically also be led by a student.

6. The last criteria is that the students are learning by playing the game and that students must feel like they are having fun by playing it—even those who might "lose." It must be played in the spirit of friendly competition, and not result in those who "lost" feeling devalued or embarrassed.

Here are some games that meet these criteria and can be adapted to all levels of instruction (and to most other subjects in addition to language). Many are "old standbys," with a few special modifications.

Games Using Small Whiteboards

Having a few small, handheld whiteboards can make a number of games go smoothly, though pieces of scratch paper can act as substitutes.

Divide the class into small groups of generally four or so students. You can change how the groups are formed—sometimes allow students to choose their own partners and at other times just have them "number off." However, always reserve the right to move students around if you feel that one group is obviously too strong or weak.

One game is calling out a question to answer or a word or sentence to spell, giving the groups twenty or thirty seconds to write the answer (telling them not to raise their board until you say time is up), and then having them show the answer. The groups with the correct answer get a point. This way everyone has an opportunity to score a point, not just the first one with the answer. Sometimes end this game, and others, with an opportunity for each team to bet all or part of their points on the last question (like in "Final Jeopardy"). Another option is for the educator to make a list of common writing errors and write them on the board (obviously, without indicating which student wrote the mistake) for groups to race to write them correctly.

A similar game with some different twists is having each group rotate having one person from their group stand up in front with a small whiteboard. All other group members have to remain in their seats. Ask questions that must be answered in writing by the person in front. However, their groups can help them by yelling out help. The first person to get the answer correct scores a point for their group. Needless to say, this game can get a little noisy.

Another game where the whiteboards come in handy is "Hangman." In this version, though you can dispense with the hanged man himself—it just adds unneeded complexity and an unnatural ending to the game itself. Have students guess entire sentences and not just words, with a space between the word blanks, and the blanks the teacher writes on the board are further distinguished by different color blanks for each word. If you're studying food, for example, instead of having to guess the word "milk," they have to guess the sentence "I drink milk in the morning." This way students can learn sentence structure and the game can easily be made harder for students with a greater grasp of the language being taught.

In this version of the "Hangman" game, students are again in groups. Give each group a turn to guess a letter, and then the educator will either write a correct letter in the appropriate blank or an incorrect letter below the blanks on the board. Groups get a point deducted if they incorrectly guess the sentence. The first group that writes the correct sentence on their whiteboard scores a point. Groups can guess the sentence at anytime, even if it is not their turn.

To help encourage that everyone is participating in these games, one option is to have the educator be the one to call on the person from each small group who shows and says the answer after everyone in the small group has discussed it.

Games That Focus on Speaking Practice

One game students enjoy is called "Telephone." In this version, divide the class into two or three groups, depending on class size. Make sure they are all seated, whisper a sentence into the first person's ear, and then, after the teacher whispers it into the ear of the first person in each group, they each have to whisper it to the next person in their group who, in turn, has to whisper it to the person next to them. The last person in the group has to come up and whisper to the teacher what the sentence is. The first group who gets it correct gets a point. If their sentence is incorrect, they have to begun the process all over again with the teacher whispering in the first person's ear. After each "turn" the "second" person becomes the one who starts the next whisper off, and the person who had begun the previous turn becomes the last.

"I Spy" is another old, but good, game. Students again are in small groups and each group has a small whiteboard. Students have to formulate questions. Every person in the group has to be prepared to ask the question because, in this game, when it's the group's turn the teacher sometimes can randomly choose who gets to ask the question ("Is it in the front of the class?" "Is it brown?"). Of course, if you do that, call on a student who you think is very likely to be able to say it correctly. Using the examples that were just given, the educator would then write "in front" or "brown" under the words "Yes" or "No" that had been written on the front board.

"Messenger and Scribe" develops both speaking and writing skills. The educator writes four sentences (or, depending on the class level, four short paragraphs) on four pieces of paper and tapes the four sheets in different sections of the room. Students are then divided into pairs—one is the Messenger and one is the Scribe. One remains seated with a paper and pen, and the other has to run back and forth between the sheets and the Scribe and tell her what it says, who then writes it down. The Messenger cannot stand by the sheet and yell to the Scribe, however. The first five or so teams to write all the sentences down correctly are the winners. Teachers should be very particular, though, on them having to get everything, including spelling and punctuation, correct.

Games That Require Students to Create Materials

There's bingo, of course, with students making a board on a piece of paper of four squares down and four squares across (they can draw the graph or be given ones that are pre-printed). They can write sixteen words out of perhaps 25 or 30 the class has been studying, and they choose which words will go in what square. Students can just tear up little pieces of paper to use as buttons to place on the words as they are called. When one person wins everyone clears their boards and plays another game.

Students can create their own word searches using graph paper. Students can exchange their creations with other students and then see who can find the most words in five minutes and then in 10 minutes.

Sentence Scrambles are also another popular game. Students are given blank index cards, or they can just cut up pieces of paper. Each student picks one sentence from a book they have been reading and writes the words and punctuation marks on the cards (one word and one punctuation mark per card). They mix up the cards and then paper clip them together. Then they do the same for another sentence. Each student can create five of them. Then collect them all, divide the class into small groups, and give each group a stack of the sentence scrambles to put into the correct order. The group that has the largest number of correct sentences in ten or fifteen minutes wins. After a group feels they have one sentence correct the educator can go check it and take the sentence scramble away after giving them a point.

In the game of Slap, students can be divided into groups of four with their desks facing each other. Each group has to make cards with one word each written on them from the week's vocabulary list. They are all put face up throughout the four desks. The teacher calls out the word, and the first person to slap the card with their hand gets a point (One person, who also plays the game, in each group is designated the scorekeeper).

Other Classroom Games

Most second-language learning classrooms have many word lists and pictures with words posted on their walls. Sometimes divide the class into small groups and give one person from each group a yardstick (they rotate who that person is). They can all start from the same point in the room and then the teacher will call out a word. The first person to correctly touch the word with their yardstick gets a point for their group. Other group members have to remain seated, but they can help their person who has the yardstick. This is another noisy game. Another alternative is writing words on the board and give students fly swatters instead of yardsticks.

Two other simple games are "Pictionary," where either students or the educator draw something on the board and the first small group to write on their white board the correct word symbolized by the drawing gets a point; and "Charades," where other students or the educator act out verbs, again needing to be guessed by student groups.

Another great game for student review can be called "Stations." Copy five copies of five different worksheets related to the theme the class has been studying (this is one of the few good uses for worksheets). The class can then be divided into five groups of four or so students. One stack of each of the five worksheets will be placed in different sections of the room. Each student group is given a group number and begins at one of the five Stations. They will be given three or four minutes (or longer) at each Station to complete as many questions on the worksheet as they can, then told to stop. They write their group number on the worksheet, give it to the teacher, and then each group moves to the next Station. After students have gone through all the Stations, each group is given another group's papers to correct and review the answers as a class. The number of correct answers is added up, and the group with the greatest number wins.

One activity that requires a little teacher preparation time is called the 'Labeling Game." The teacher can write words describing various classroom objects on post-its, divide the classroom into four or five groups, and then each day during the week one group will see how fast they can correctly label the classroom objects. The groups are timed, and the one with the fastest time wins. Additional labels are added each week.

Online Games

There are several online games that meet the criteria laid out at the beginning of this appendix. These are free learning games (most offer a choice of subjects—English, Math, Science or History) where classes can immediately create private "virtual rooms" where students are competing against all the other students in the class—but not with anyone else. The three best are from the BBC—Gut Instinct (<http://www.bbc.co.uk/schools/ks2bitesize/games/gut_instinct/pop.shtml>); Mia Cadaver's Tombstone Timeout (<http://www.bbc.co.uk/schools/gcsebitesize/games/mia/index.shtml>); and Elemental (<http://www.bbc.co.uk/schools/ks3bitesize/game/elemental/index.shtml>).

The other issue that goes with these games relates to the award the winners and, often, the "runner-ups," receive. The rewards can cost the teacher little or nothing—an extra point on that week's test, students get to go to lunch two minutes early, or they don't have to do the required work of copying the plan for the day in their notebook. Sometimes it's a piece of candy, or the right to eat food during class.

But, generally, after a short period of time you'll find that students forget about getting a reward and don't even ask about it. The game itself becomes the reward, and the enjoyment of the experience and the knowledge learned becomes the intrinsic motivator.

Works Cited

Alinsky, Saul. *Rules for Radicals*. New York: Vintage Books, 1971.

Alliance for Excellent Education. "Urgent but Overlooked: The Literacy Crisis among Adolescent English Language Learners." February 2007. <http://www.all4ed.org/files/Urgent Over.pdf>.

Arendt, Hannah. *Eichmann in Jerusalem: A Report on the Banality of Evil*. New York: Penguin Books, 2006.

Bassano, Sharron. *Sounds Easy! Phonics, Spelling, and Pronunciation Practice*. Burlingame, CA: Alta Book Center Publishers, 2002.

Bennis, Warren, and Naus, Burt. *Leaders*. New York: Harper & Row Publishers, 1985.

Bergin, Christi, and Bergin, D. "Relationships Improve Student Success." *Science Daily* 30 June 2009. <http://www.sciencedaily.com/releases/2009/06/090630132009.htm>.

Boaler, Jo. "Learning from Teaching: Exploring the Relationship between Reform Curriculum and Equity." *Journal for Research in Mathematics Education* 33.4 (2002): 239–58.

Bowman, Brenda, Larson, Mary Jo, Short, Deborah, McKay, Heather, and Valdez-Pierce, Lorraine. *Teaching English as a Foreign Language to Large Multilevel Classes*. Washington, DC: Peace Corps Collection and Information Exchange Division, 1992.

Branch, Taylor. *Parting the Waters: America in the King Years 1954–63*. New York: Simon & Schuster, 1988.

Bruner, Jerome. *Acts of Meaning*. Cambridge, MA: Harvard College, 1992.

Bruner, Jerome. *The Culture of Education*. Cambridge, MA: Harvard UP, 1996.

Burke, Jim. *The English Teacher's Companion*. Portsmouth, NH: Heinemann, 2003.

Caine, Renat Nummela, and Caine, Geoffrey. *Making Connections: Teaching and the Human Brain*. Menlo Park, CA: Addison Wesley, 1994.

Calhoun, Emily F. *Teaching Beginning Reading and Writing with the Picture Word Inductive Model*. Alexandria, VA: Association For Supervision and Curriculum Development, 1999.

Calhoun, Emily F., Poirier, Tracy, Simon, Nicole, and Mueller, Lisa. "Teacher (and District) Research: Three Inquiries into the Picture Word Inductive Model." Annual Meeting of the American Educational Research Association, Seattle, Washington, 10–14 April 2001.

Colombo, Louis. "Action Strategies For Community Development." Neighborhood Planning, 9 August 2009. <http://www.neighborhoodplanning.org/pdf/ActionStrategiesforCommunity Dvlpmt.pdf>.

Covey, Stephen. *7 Habits of Highly Effective People*. New York: Simon & Schuster, 1990.

Dale, Edgar. *Audio-visual Methods in Teaching.* New York: Dryden, 1969.

Dantas-Whitney, Maria. *Critical Reflection in the Second Language Classroom through Audiotaped Journals.* Corvallis, OR: Oregon State University, 2002.

Deci, Edward. *Why We Do What We Do.* New York: Penguin Books, 1995.

Dewey, John. *Democracy and Education.* New York: The Macmillan Company, 1916.

Dictionary.com. "Judgment." 3 August 2009. <http://dictionary.reference.com/browse/judgment>.

Dictionary.com. "Opinion." <http://dictionary.reference.com/browse/opinion>.

Drucker, Peter. *Management: Tasks, Responsibilities, Practices.* New York: Harper & Row, 1974.

Drucker, Peter. *The Effective Executive.* London: Butterworth-Heinemann, 2007.

Eliot, T. S. "The Dry Salvages." *The Four Quartets.* <http://www.tristan.icom43.net/quartets/salvages.html>

Erwin, Jonathan. *The Classroom of Choice.* Alexandria, VA: ASCD Books, 1999.

eSchool News. "School Laptop Program Begets Writing Gains." *eSchool News.* 2 February 2008. <http://www.eschoolnews.com/2008/02/04/school-laptop-program-begets-writing-gains/>.

Fellner, Terry, and Apple, Matthew. "Developing Writing Fluency and Lexical Complexity with Blogs." *The JALT CALL Journal* 2 (2006): 15–26.

Ferlazzo, Larry, and Hammond, Lorie. *Building Parent Engagement in School.* Santa Barbara, CA: Linworth Publishing, 2009.

Fichtman Dana, Nancy, and Yendol-Hoppey, Diane. *The Reflective Educator's Guide to Classroom Research.* Thousand Oaks, CA: Corwin Press, 2009.

Glasser, William. *Choice Theory in the Classroom.* New York: Harper Perennial, 1988.

Greenwood, Charles R., Arreaga-Mayer, Carmen, Utley, Cheryl A., Gavin, Karen M., and Terry, Barbara J. "ClassWide Peer Tutoring Learning Management System." *Remedial and Special Education* 22 (2001): 34–47.

Griffiths, Carol (Ed.). *Lessons from Good Language Learners.* Cambridge, UK: Cambridge UP, 2008.

Haight, Carrie, Herron, Carol, and Cole, Seven. "The Effects of Deductive and Guided Inductive Instructional Approaches on the Learning of Grammar in the Elementary Foreign Language College Classroom." *Foreign Language Annals* 40.2 (2008): 288–310.

Haroutunian-Gordon, Sophie. *Turning the Soul.* Chicago, IL: University of Chicago Press, 1991.

Hatton, Neville, and Smith, David. "Reflection in Teacher Education: Towards Definition and Implementation." 1995. <http://alex.edfac.usyd.edu.au/LocalResource/Study1/hattonart.html>.

Hmelo-Silver, Cindy E., Duncan, Ravit G., and Chinn, Clark A. "Scaffolding and Achievement in Problem-Based and Inquiry Learning: A Response to Kirschner, Sweller, and Clark." *Educational Psychologist* 42.2 (2007): 99–107.

Horton, Myles, and Freire, Paulo. *We Make the Road by Walking.* Philadelphia, PA: Temple University Press, 1990.

Jensen, Eric. *Brain Based Learning.* San Diego, CA: The Brain Store, 2000.

Johnson, David, Johnson, Roger, and Roseth, Cary. "Do Peer Relationships Affect Achievement?" Cooperative Learning Institute. 9 March 2006. <http://www.co-operation.org/pages/news letter2006.doc>.

Jones, Jami. "Building Resiliency." Ask Dr. Jami. 2006. <http://www.askdrjami.org/resiliency/ buildingresiliency.html>.

Joyce, Bruce, and Calhoun, Emily. *Learning to Teach Inductively.* Boston, MA: Allyn Bacon, 1998.

Krashen, Stephen. "Applying the Comprehension Hypothesis: Some Suggestions." 13th International Symposium and Book Fair on Language Teaching, Taipei, Taiwan. November 2004.

Krashen, Stephen. "Free Voluntary Reading: New Research, Applications, and Controversies." RELC Conference, Singapore, April, 2004. <http://www.sdkrashen.com/articles/singapore/singapore. pdf>.

Krashen, Stephen. *Principles and Practice in Second Language Acquisition.* Upper Saddle River, NJ: Prentice-Hall, 1981.

Krashen, Stephen. "Second Language Acquisition and Second Language Learning." 2002. <http:// www.sdkrashen.com/SL_Acquisition_and_Learning/index.html>.

Lantolf, James, and Appel, Gabriela. *Vygotskian Approaches to Second Language Research.* Westport, CT: Ablex Publishing, 1994.

Marzano, Robert J. *The Art and Science of Teaching.* Alexandria, VA: ASCD, 2007.

Mathews-Aydinli, Julie. "Problem-Based Learning and Adult English Language Learners." Center for Adult English Language Acquisition, Center for Applied Linguistics. April 2007. <http://www. cal.org/caela/esl_resources/briefs/Problem-based.pdf>.

Menchin, Scott. *Taking a Bath with the Dog and Other Things That Make Me Happy.* Cambridge, MA: Candlewick, 2007.

Mergendoller, John R., Maxwell, Nan L., and Bellisimo, Yolanda. "The Effectiveness of Problem-Based Instruction: A Comparative Study of Instructional Methods and Student Characteristics." *The Interdisciplinary Journal of Problem Based Learning* 1.2 (2006): 49–69.

National Capital Language Resource Center. "High School Foreign Language Students' Perceptions of Language Learning Strategies Use and Self-Efficacy." 1996. <http://www.nclrc.org/about_ teaching/reports_pub/high_school_fls_perceptions.pdf>.

Palmer, Adrian S., Rodgers, Theodore S., and Winn-Bell Olsen, Judy. *Back and Forth: Photocopiable Cooperative Pair Activities for Language Development.* San Francisco, CA: Alta Book Center Publishers, 1990.

Pollard, Laurel. *Zero Prep for Beginners.* Burlingame, CA: ESL Books, 2001.

Rholheiser, Carol, and Ross, John. "Student Self-Evaluation: What Research Says and What Practice Shows." <http://www.cdl.org/resource-library/articles/self_eval.php?type=subject&id=4>.

Rodgers, Carol. "Defining Reflection: Another Look at John Dewey and Reflective Thinking." *Teachers College Record* 104.4 (2002): 842–66.

Rogers, Spence, Ludington, Jim, and Graham, Shari. *Motivation and Learning.* Evergreen, CO: Peak Learning Systems, 1999.

Ryan, Kevin, and Cooper, James M. *Those Who Can, Teach,* 12th edition. Belmont, CA: Wadsworth Publishing, 2008.

Schank, Roger. *Tell Me a Story.* New York: Scribner's Sons, 1990.

Schütz, Ricardo. "Stephen Krashen's Theory of Second Language Acquisition." *English Made in Brazil.* 2 July 2007. <http://www.sk.com.br/sk-krash.html>.

Srimavin, Wilaksana, and Darasawang, Pornapit. "Developing Self-Assessment through Journal Writing." Proceedings of the Independent Learning Conference 2003. Independent Learning, September 2004. <http://independentlearning.org/ILA/ila03/ila03_srimavin_and_pornapit.pdf?q=ila03/ila03_srimavin_and_pornapit.pdf>.

Starkman, Neal, Roberts, Clay, and Scales, Peter C. *Great Places to Learn.* Minneapolis, MN: The Search Institute, Search Institute Press, 2006.

Stern, Hans H. *Fundamental Concepts of Language Teaching.* Oxford: Oxford UP, 1983.

Suarez-Orozco, Carola, Pimentel, Allyson, and Martin, Margary. "The Significance of Relationships: Academic Engagement and Achievement among Newcomer Immigrant Youth." *Teachers College Record* 111.3 (2009): 712–49.

Truscott, John. "The Case against Grammar Correction in L2 Writing Classes." *Language Learning* 46.2 (1996): 327–69.

Viadero, Debra. "Peer Tutoring's Potential to Boost IQ Intrigues Educators." *Education Week.* 7 October 2007. <http://www.edweek.org/login.html?source=http://www.edweek.org/ew/articles/2007/10/03/06peertutor.h27.html&destination=http://www.edweek.org/ew/articles/2007/10/03/06peertutor.h27.html&levelId=2100>.

Waxman, Hersholt C., Freiberg, H. Jerome, Vaughn, Joseph C., and Weil, Marsha (Eds.). *Images of Reflection in Teacher Education.* Reston, VA: Association of Teacher Educators, 1988.

Willis, Judy. *Research-Based Strategies to Ignite Student Learning.* Alexandria, VA: ASCD, 2006.

Wormeli, Rick. *Summarization in Any Subject.* Alexandria, VA: ASCD Books, 2005.

Zehr, Mary A. "Hurdles Remain High for English-Learners." *Education Week.* 4 June 2008. <http://www.edweek.org/login.html?source=http://www.edweek.org/ew/articles/2008/06/04/39sacramento_ep.h27.html&destination=http://www.edweek.org/ew/articles/2008/06/04/39sacramento_ep.h27.html&levelId=2100>.

Index